Martial Arts™

the
Karate
handbook

Martial Arts™

the Karate
handbook

Ray Pawlett

ROSEN
PUBLISHING

New York

New Lenox
Public Library District
120 Veterans Parkway
New Lenox, Illinois 60451

This North American edition published in 2008 by:

The Rosen Publishing Group, Inc.
29 East 21st Street
New York, NY 10010

North American edition, this format, printed in 2008
by The Rosen Publishing Group, Inc.

Creative Director: Sarah King
Technical Consultant: Glenn Stevens
Project Editor: Clare Haworth-Maden
Photographer: Colin Bowling
Designer: Axis Design Editions

Library of Congress Cataloging-in-Publication Data

Pawlett, Ray.
The karate handbook / Ray Pawlett.
    p. cm. — (Martial arts)
Includes bibliographical references and index.
ISBN-13: 978-1-4042-1394-4 (library binding)
1. Karate—Juvenile literature. I. Pawlett, Raymond.
II. Title.
GV1114.3.P39 2008
796.815'3—dc22
                                                2007032795

Manufactured in the China

contents

introduction

During the mid–1990s, I was fortunate that my martial-arts career introduced me to shoto kan karate under the instruction of Sensei John Van Weenen in the middle regions of Great Britain. I found the Sensei a wealth of information about a traditional form of karate that was both practical and theoretically stimulating.

This was my introduction to Japanese culture. My search for knowledge eventually led me in the direction of shiatsu (a Japanese healing art often practiced by the karate masters) and tai chi (a Chinese martial art).

We never know exactly where our paths will lead.

Mine was not to become an expert in karate itself, but more of a martial artist and healer. This has given me a deep and wide understanding of the martial arts and some of the deeper, more spiritual aspects that they embrace. It was therefore with great pleasure that I accepted the challenge of writing a karate handbook.

What seems to matter is that while on your individual sections of the path, you immerse yourself in the moment and learn your lessons from that moment. Learning karate not only pointed me toward some life-enriching choices, but taught me how deep the well of learning from the Far East is. For this, I shall be eternally grateful.

With this in mind, I would like to dedicate this book to all seekers who follow the path of the martial artist or healing. Good luck, and enjoy the path!

Karate teaches you to be precise with your body movements.

a word of warning

The techniques in this book have been selected from traditional karate training and modern scientific sports training. Every effort has been made to try to ensure that all of the techniques and methods described are accurate and safe.

Karate is a physical art. In every physical-movement skill, whether it is martial arts, dance, or sports, there is an element of risk. Ultimately, the person who is responsible for managing that risk is you.

It is all too easy to misunderstand the written word slightly. This could result in injury if you are unlucky. Also, the exercises and training tips in this book may not suit your individual requirements. For this reason, it is vital that you consult your instructor before taking up the training described in this book. If you are still in doubt, consult a doctor or appropriately qualified person.

The techniques and applications described are real. Under no circumstances should you attempt the two-person training techniques unless your instructor agrees that you are ready to do so.

Conversely, the techniques are techniques that require training. Even the most basic-looking technique will have multiple layers of complexity. Do not think that reading a karate book teaches you self-defense. For that you will need qualified instruction. Always try to walk away from a self-defense situation if you can.

chapter 1 **what is karate?**

Karate is a Japanese martial art. It is practiced by millions of people around the world of all ages, races, and physical abilities. It is equally suitable for men and women as it relies on technique rather than pure physical strength.

Karate has developed in many different ways. It can be looked upon as an art form, a spiritual path, a sport, a self-defense system, a fitness routine, or all of these things. Underneath this myriad of reflections lies the essence of karate.

Karate has its roots in the traditional jujitsu of Japan, and specifically Okinawa, roots that have never been forgotten.

Karate emphasizes strikes and blocks. The strikes and blocks can be made with many different parts of the body. One of the lessons of karate is how to use different parts of your body to attack or defend to the maximum advantage. The advanced karate student will also be able to employ locks, strangles, and throws.

Respect and courtesy are integral parts of the teachings of karate. Karate students must learn respect for themselves, others, and the world at large.

Karate has its philosophical roots in Zen Buddhism. The ways of Zen permeate through the whole of the strategy and framework of karate. It can be said that on many levels, the study of karate is the study of Zen Buddhism. Karate is therefore inherently peaceful, and the final opponent that one always meets before making any improvements is oneself.

martial arts

If you imagine a caveman crawling out of his cave into the wide world, the first thing that he is going to think about is feeding himself. So our humble caveman manages to find some food and is lucky enough to store some away.

Now, as with any animal, some will try to collect their own food and others will try to steal it from them. After having had his food stolen a few times, our caveman is becoming accustomed to defending his patch. In other words, he is learning to defend himself, or is learning a martial skill.

Then he meets other cavemen who are in the same predicament. With what communication skills they have, they swap what they have learned about defending themselves. Each member of the group improves his skill by exchanging information with his allies. The group shares information and develops a martial style that is unique to that individual group.

We will now skip a few hundred thousand years. The descendant of our original caveman

Martial arts should be a spiritual path, as well as a physical one.

has become more sophisticated. He is still defending his food in a manner of speaking, but this time he is being paid by the people who collect the food to protect them from others who may wish to steal it. In other words, he has become a professional soldier or warrior.

But his society is not the only thing that has developed. Man's internal thought processes and brain have altered over the millennia. Our warrior is no longer the instinctual creature that our caveman was.

Our warrior has to use his skill to defend his people. He has had to kill people and has seen his comrades killed. That sort of thing can change the way that you think about your own life and death. These thoughts will naturally turn inward. Without some kind of spiritual framework, the thoughts become fears. With a spiritual framework, the fear of death is no longer a paralyzing sensation, but something that can be managed.

In this way, the warriors of the tribes naturally needed the skills of the spiritual guides of the tribes. In some instances, the way of the warrior became a spiritual path. We now have what could be called a martial art instead of a martial skill.

It will not take long for the warrior to think that there are many other ways to solve a situation other than fighting. The warrior's outlook on life becomes more peaceful. He understands that the biggest fight is not with his enemies, but controlling himself. He is now on a quest for inner peace.

Japan and Okinawa

This is, of course, a very basic way of describing the evolution of the martial arts. However, it does illustrate that there is a difference between learning a martial art and just learning how to be a good fighter.

That is not to say that a good fighter is a bad person or cannot be a spiritual person. The great boxer Mohammed Ali was also a person of strong spiritual inclinations, while the poet Byron was said to be a good boxer!

The difference between the martial artist and the fighter tends to be that the martial artist is more interested in some kind of inner development that goes beyond learning how to fight.

Karate comes from Japan. To be more precise, what we know as karate actually originated on a small island near Japan called Okinawa. When trying to understand the history of karate, it is useful to have a good idea of where Okinawa is in relationship to Japan and China.

Okinawa is a small Japanese island measuring about 6 miles (10 kilometers) wide by about 42 miles (110km) long. It is the main island in the Ryuku group of islands that spans from China to Japan. It is nearly equidistant between China, Japan, and Taiwan. During its history, it developed into an important resting spot and trading post between China, Japan, Taiwan, Thailand, Malaysia, Borneo, and the Philippines. Indeed, the commercial importance of Okinawa's position was also seen as having strategic importance during World War II. It was the site of the famous battle for Sugar Loaf Hill that lasted for ten days.

Knowing the position of Okinawa is important because it helps one to understand the different influences that combined to create karate.

Farming and fishing are the principal industries of Okinawa, although the biggest export by far must be karate.

CHINA

JAPAN

OKINAWA

the history of karate

According to legend, a Buddhist monk named Bodidharma walked barefoot from India to China. When in China, he found a temple called Shaolin–Si ("small forest temple") and taught the monks Zen Buddhism. Part of his teaching was an exercise system that could be used to defend oneself. This is how the very famous shaolin style of kung fu is said to have evolved. Shaolin kung fu became the base upon which many of the Chinese martial arts were developed.

As we have seen, the island of Okinawa lies on an important trading route between China and Japan. The Okinawans had their own form of martial-arts training. The style of the martial art varied between the small towns on the island. (Do not forget how small the island is.) The variations tended to be along the lines of emphasizing different movements rather than changing actual movements.

The martial style of Okinawa was known as "te," or "the empty hand." The regional variations were collectively known as Okinawa–te.

Now, as history has often shown, if you are living on a small island on an important trading route, you are in a spot that is likely to be invaded. During the thirteenth century, the Japanese took over the island and then banned the carrying of weapons. Then the influence of the Chinese styles of martial art made itself known. As the Chinese styles that were adopted were bare-hand forms of combat, the carrying of weapons was no longer a requirement.

An interesting legend about this time tells that much of the training was done at night, when the Japanese shogun was sleeping. It is said that the training clothes used were also sleeping clothes. Hence the birth of the karate suit, or gi.

This fighting style became known as "tode," or "the Chinese hand." The Chinese character for tode can also be pronounced "kara." This was coupled with the original "te" and so the word

A Japanese banner for a karate school.

"karate" was invented. The original meaning of the word "karate" was thus "the Chinese hand."

Later, the karate master Gichin Funakoshi adopted the alternative meaning of the Chinese character kara, which is "empty," and added the word "do" to the name. The word "do" means "path" or "way." The name "karate do" had been born, meaning "the way of the empty hand."

The idea of "do" was not new. If you read Buddhist writings from times long predating Funakoshi, it is clear that the concept had always been there. The "way" that is implied is a spiritual path toward enlightenment.

Nearly every sport, science, martial art, or art form has a person in its history who is said to have brought it to the world and revolutionized it. In karate, we have Gichin Funakoshi.

Gichin Funakoshi was an Okinawan who was born in 1868 and died in 1957. He was taught martial arts in the beginning by many of the most notable Okinawan martial artists, including Azato and Itosu.

Gichin Funakoshi, like many other martial artists, was not a particularly strong child. When of elementary-school age, Master Azato taught him the ways of the martial arts and improved his strength. Funakoshi was also an intelligent child who became well read in many of the classics of Chinese and Japanese knowledge.

In 1917, Funakoshi traveled from Okinawa to Kyoto to give his first martial-arts demonstration at the request of the Japanese Ministry for Education. A few years later, in 1921, he gave another demonstration to Crown Prince Hirohito at Shuri Castle. The crown prince was highly impressed with the display.

In 1922, Dr. Jigoro Kano (the founder of judo) invited Funakoshi to teach karate at the Kodokan Dojo, a famous place of martial-arts learning at the time. This allowed Funakoshi to become established in Japan and his karate to get a foothold in the country.

Eventually, Funakoshi was able to afford his own dojo, or training hall. Funakoshi had the nickname Shoto, meaning "waving pines." The Japanese word for hall is "kan." The two words were put together, so that people were said to train at Shotokan, or "Shoto's hall." The word "shotokan" became synonymous with his training style and was adopted as the name for that style of karate.

While it is true that Funakoshi was the originator of the shotokan style, it was his son, Yoshitaka Funakoshi, who developed it into the form that we know today. It seems that the father developed the system and the son understood how to teach the system and bring it to the people.

In 1922, Hironori Ohtsuka (1892–1982) began studying karate with Funakoshi. He had already had a long training in jujitsu before meeting Funakoshi. In 1939, he started his own style and called it wado ryu. "Wado ryu" translates as "the way of harmony." In wado ryu, to show aggression is discouraged. For this reason, it is sometimes translated as "the peaceful way."

The symbol of the wado ryu school of karate.

Wado ryu combines the basic movements of jujitsu with techniques of evasion, putting a strong emphasis on softness.

Another karate style that originated in Okinawa was goju–ryu. The style was developed by Kanryo Higaonna (1853–1915), who opened a school on the island. The core of his teaching stems from eight forms that he brought from China. His top student, Chojun Miyagi (1888–1953), founded the goju–ryu style in 1930. "Goju–ryu" means "hard–soft way." The emphasis in goju–ryu is upon soft, circular blocking techniques, with a strong counterattack being quickly delivered.

Shito–ryu was founded in 1928 by Kenwa Mabuni (1889–1952), and was directly influenced by the Okinawan styles. The name "shito" is constructed from the names of Mabuni's teachers, Ankoh Itosu and Kanryo Higaonna. The style uses a large number of kata (around fifty) and emphasizes power in the execution of the techniques.

As you can see from the dates given for these styles, they have all been developed relatively recently. In one way or another, most of the modern karate styles can be traced back to Gichin Funakoshi. For this reason, he is sometimes called "the grandfather of karate." His memorial bears the phrase "There is no first attack in karate," emphasizing his peaceful nature.

Karate continues to develop as it did in the days of Funakoshi. Nowadays, there are many different styles, so I apologize if I have missed yours! Each style has its own emphasis and tactical method. But one thing can be said about *all* of the styles: the goal is the same, namely that of spiritual peace and harmony. A common phrase used to describe the styles is that they are all "paths up the same mountain."

In 1964, an attempt was made to formulate a set of rules that would encompass all of the styles so that competitions could be held between the styles by the Federation of All Japan Karate–do Organization (FAJKO). In 1970, the first "all-styles" karate world championships were held in Tokyo. At the same time, a meeting was held and the World Union of Karate–do Organizations was formed.

The diversity of styles makes it impossible for us to look at them all in this book. Instead, we shall look at many of the techniques that are common to all styles, although the execution may vary. We shall also look at some of the kata from the shotokan style.

other martial-arts styles

These days, people practice a bewildering number of martial-arts styles. Many of them can be traced back to either karate or something that influenced karate, although certainly not all of them.

We will now take a quick look at some of them so that we can get an idea of their differences. It is good to have an idea of where karate lies in the martial-arts spectrum.

jujitsu

Jujitsu is another Japanese martial art. The literal translation is that "ju" means "soft" and "jitsu" in this sense means "art." So jujitsu means "the art of softness." This does not mean that people who practice jujitsu are soft, however!

"Soft" in this sense means that you yield to an attack. Instead of trying to knock an attack out of the way, you yield to it and redirect it.

Jujitsu is the martial art of the samurai, and is consequently the elder brother of all of the other Japanese martial arts. It has therefore taken on the samurai code of honor and much of its philosophy.

If you imagine a samurai warrior in battle, it is possible that he may become separated from his sword. He will still have to go on fighting, however, otherwise he will die. Jujitsu is the unarmed samurai's form of combat. For this reason, many of the traditional jujitsu techniques are designed to "finish" an opponent swiftly and efficiently.

As a style, jujitsu includes just about everything from the unarmed-combat repertoire. It has kicks, blocks, strikes, and punches, similar to karate. It contains many of the throws, locks, and strangleholds that are used in judo, too. It also contains many techniques, such as neck

locks, that would not be safe to use on the judo mat.

As you can imagine, jujitsu has a very wide scope. Different masters emphasized different areas in training. Some would use harder techniques; others would use soft, circular techniques. There could be an emphasis on strikes or an emphasis on locks. This is why several different styles of jujitsu are practiced around the world.

judo

Judo has its roots in jujitsu. During the nineteenth century, jujitsu had gained a somewhat undesirable reputation. Basically, the wrong people were practicing it and using it for the wrong reasons.

Jigoro Kano was a successful jujitsu student of the time. He had studied the art in many of the best Japanese schools and had a good understanding of it. He saw that the art that he loved could easily be destroyed by those with less of a sense of responsibility than him.

What he set out to do was to take the best from the jujitsu routines and to make them safe as a challenging training routine for the mind and body. What he ended up with was judo.

"Judo," the name of his new system, means "gentle way." The philosophy of the movement is to use your opponent's energy against him or her, and it is therefore a very efficient style of martial art.

All of the kicks, strikes, and dangerous locks were removed from the jujitsu routine to create the judo system. The new judo system was now suitable for tournaments and competitions.

Judo is a sophisticated wrestling style that incorporates the honor, philosophy, and respect of the martial arts. It is easily recognizable from the throws and groundwork that it incorporates.

It is a very popular martial art that is watched by millions worldwide as an Olympic event, and that has students of all ages, sizes, and abilities, as well as of both sexes, throughout the world.

aikido

Aikido is another Japanese martial art. The style was founded by Morihei Ueshiba (1883–1966).

Ueshiba studied under a martial-arts master called Takeda from 1912 until 1919. He learned a variety of different techniques that had been formalized by the Aizu clan. The style was called daito ryu–aiki jujutsu. It is possible to trace this style back to the sixth century.

After studying with Takeda for seven years, Ueshiba devoted the next six years of his life to studying a spiritual tradition under Onisaburo Deguchi. He traveled throughout Asia with Kyo, working with the discipline.

In 1927, Ueshiba started a dojo in Tokyo, teaching a mixture of the martial-arts traditions that he had learned from Takeda and the spiritual tradition that he learned from Deguchi.

Ueshiba was eventually to call this new style of teaching "aikido." "Ai" means harmony, "ki" stands for the universal life force, and "do" is "the way." "Aikido" therefore translates as "the way of harmonizing spirit."

In aikido, you harmonize with an attack. You do not try to deflect an attack, but instead draw it in toward you and neutralize it by redirecting it into a throw, joint lock, or another technique.

Aikido is classified as a "soft" style because it uses soft, circular, blocking movements in a similar way that tai chi does.

The aikido student will not usually enter competitions because there are no competitions in traditional aikido. This is fitting, for Ueshiba's idea was that aikido is not learning how to defeat others, but how to defeat the negative characteristics that lie within all of us.

In aikido, you "blend" with your attacker.

tai chi

Tai chi is a Chinese martial art. Its relevance to karate is that it influenced all of the other Chinese martial arts. And, as we know, the Chinese martial arts were a major influence on the Okinawan martial arts that karate came from. Reference is made to this influence in the "chinte" pattern, or Chinese pattern, that is taught in some karate schools.

Tai chi has existed in different forms since at least the thirteenth century. During the seventeenth century, much tai-chi knowledge was formulized by the Chen family. During the nineteenth century, another style derived from the Chen style was founded by Yang Lu Chan. Yang Lu Chan's "yang"-style tai chi was popularized by his grandson, Yang Chen Fu, during the early twentieth century.

Tai chi and aikido use very similar techniques that are executed in a slightly different way. The main rationale behind both is the concept of yin and yang. The idea is that you use the interplay of opposites. If a hard force is coming toward you, you become soft and yield. This makes attackers overextend their bodies so that you can control them.

Tai chi is characterized by slow, graceful movements performed in a meditative manner, but beneath the aesthetic appeal is a martial-art style as deadly as any of the others.

Practitioners of tai chi use soft, circular movements.

tae kwon do

Tae kwon do is recognizable by its emphasis on high kicks.

In 1910, the Japanese invaded Korea and banned the practice of Korean martial arts. The Koreans tend to be very patriotic people who see their martial arts as their heritage, so, as you can imagine, tae kwon do went underground.

In 1945, Korea regained its independence and tae kwon do enjoyed a resurgence. The Japanese occupation had had an effect upon tae kwon do in that its practitioners had adopted some karate techniques.

In 1958, the tae kwon do masters Song Duk Ki and Sung Hwan gave a demonstration to the Korean president. The intention of this demonstration was to reestablish tae kwon do as a martial art that is different from karate and can stand alone. Tae kwon do had regained its identity.

Since then, tae kwon do has gone from strength to strength and is now an Olympic sport.

To the uninitiated, tae kwon do can look very similar to karate. The outfits worn look the same, and tae kwon do emphasizes kicking and punching in the sparring rather than throws and locks. There are differences, however. Usually, tae kwon do experts place a greater emphasis on kicking. There is also a difference in approach: tae kwon do stems more from Taoism, and karate, from Zen Buddhism. These differences have resulted in subtle changes in the teaching and in the execution of some of the moves.

Tae kwon do is an ancient martial art that originated in Korea. Old manuscripts and paintings suggest that a form of martial art was practiced here as long as two thousand years ago. The style has changed its name over the ages, and has undoubtedly changed the way that it looks, too, but its origins are very old.

the roots of karate

So now we understand that karate has been around for a long time, even though it was not actually called "karate" by Gichin Funakoshi until the beginning of the twentieth century.

I have mentioned concepts like Zen and spirituality and have said that they were vital to the inception of the karate style. Much karate training is based on traditional methods, although the methods do take new knowledge on board as and when it comes along.

It makes sense, then, to look at what we mean by some of these concepts. With a little more effort, you will be able to understand them rather than just being able to repeat them. This will not make a visible difference to your karate, but will alter how your karate feels, and an experienced instructor will notice the change.

Zen Buddhism

The story goes that Bodidharma crossed India to teach Zen Buddhism and exercises at the Shaolin temple in China, and that his influence spread to the martial arts in Japan.

If Bodidharma did exist, he was certainly not the only one practicing Zen Buddhism. If you take a look at Japanese culture, you will see Zen influences in its paintings, food, archery, martial arts, and calligraphy, for instance. The famous Japanese tea ceremony is an example of a Zen ritual. The name of the tea ceremony is "cha–do," or the "way of tea." It is the same "do" that is referred to in "karate–do."

Another name for Zen is "dhyana." This name implies meditation, although the disciplines of meditation are less strict than those of other Buddhist practices. Zen is not actually a religion in the sense that a deity is worshipped, although some Zen monasteries and schools use their understanding of the discipline like a microscope to examine their own souls.

So what is Zen? This is a difficult question to answer because Zen is not a set of rules. It is more of an experience. A traditional way to gain insights into Zen is by studying the Japanese poetry form called haiku. Haiku's short poems attempt to crystallize the essence of Zen in three lines of verse.

Here is a typical example by the Japanese Zen master Sogyo, who lived between 1667 and 1731.

Careful! Even moonlit dew drops,
If you're lured to watch,
Are a wall before the truth

As you can see, this short poem is very illuminating about the nature of Zen. In Zen, you are trying to find a truth that is never far away. It is straight in front of us, and may become clear at any moment. It is a truth that lies beyond beauty (indeed, the warning implicit in the poem is not to be fooled by beauty).

So how does this apply to karate? In his book *Zen and the Art of Archery*, the author Eugen Herrigel describes a time when he joined a Zen school to learn archery. In the school, he was asked to practice drawing a bow until the bow drew itself. This seemed like a paradox. He was being asked to practice a skill so diligently that he did not even know that he was using it.

I sometimes think of it as a skilled craftsman using his tools. The craftsman has spent years learning his skill and performs it effortlessly. But if you were to use the same tools, you would not succeed unless you were lucky.

Karate is like that. You need to practice your skills until you get to the point where you do not need to use them. In tournaments, winners will not tell you that they saw an opening and placed a kick. What they are more likely to tell you is that they just kicked and got the point. That is a Zen concept in karate.

an old samurai story

Here is an old story about a samurai warrior named Miyamoto Mushashi. He was the author of a book called *The Book of Five Rings*, dating from 1643. It is a fascinating book to read if you want an insight into the workings of the samurai mind.

The samurai were the warrior caste of Japan. They are well known even today for their strict code of honor. If this code of honor were to be broken, the penalty could even be death.

Mushashi was said to be the best swordsman of all of the samurai. He would teach new samurai his ways, and *The Book of Five Rings* was his attempt to convey some of his teachings by means of the written word.

Being the best fighter is not always a good thing to be. It puts you in a position in which others who want to prove themselves the best warrior will want to challenge you.

According to the code of the samurai, such a challenge would have to be accepted and would result in a fight to the death. Mushashi had received many such challenges, and had won them all. You can just imagine him trying to teach new warriors and someone from another school coming and laying down a challenge.

After some time, he no longer wanted to be a part of these killings, and therefore decided to exile himself. He chose to build a home on a small island and to live the life of a fisherman.

If anything, this just made his legend stronger. Young warriors would search all over Japan for Mushashi, but couldn't find him. Eventually, however, one of them learned the name of the island on which he was living and went to seek him out.

Now that he was living his life as a fisherman, Mushashi was less concerned about how he looked to the world. His hair had become long and white and he had grown a beard.

Our challenger reaches the island and cannot locate Mushashi. He does, however, find an old fisherman bringing in his daily catch. The old man is actually Mushashi, but the young warrior does not recognize him because of his changed appearance.

He asks the old man the whereabouts of Mushashi, and proudly tells him that he is going to fight Mushashi and become known as the greatest warrior in Japan. The old man says that he knows Mushashi, and that he has given up the ways of the sword. But the young warrior is not deterred and declares that he must fight for his honor.

By this time, Mushashi has brought in his boat and has an oar in his hand. He hits the challenger over the head with the oar, thereby killing him.

This story is relevant to the study of karate because it describes the warrior spirit. The old man had tried to show mercy and had pleaded with the challenger to abandon his quest, but to no avail. Instead of waiting for the challenger to take the advantage, Mushashi realized that he had the advantage and used it, to the challenger's loss. If the challenger had shown more respect and mercy to the old man, he would have lived longer.

ki

According to the philosophies of the East, there is an energy field that transforms our bodies from sacks of chemicals into living entities. The Japanese call this energy field "ki," the Chinese, "chi," while the Indian yogis call it "prana."

It is this same energy that a shiatsu (energy-massage) practitioner or an acupuncturist will use to try to heal a patient or client. The theory is that if the ki in your body can flow evenly, then you will be healthy. But if the ki becomes blocked, or cannot flow for some reason, illness can set in.

Shiatsu therapists use their touch to try to distribute the flow of ki evenly. Acupuncturists do the same using needles. Both techniques have become very popular in the West in recent years.

Shiatsu and martial arts have been linked for many years through their connection with ki. Many of the great karate masters also had a good understanding of shiatsu, or at least an instinctive feel for the subject. Why do you think that this is?

The reason is that ki can be used for whatever your intent wants. If you want to use it to heal, then your mind will be in a very different state to that should you want to hurt someone. In both instances, you will have projected your ki, but the intention of your mind rules the way that it works.

If you want a demonstration of how ki works, think about the karateka who break pieces of wood with their strikes. If you are hitting a piece of wood, you do not aim *at* the piece of wood, you aim *through* the piece of wood. If you aim at the wood, you hurt your hand. If you aim through the wood, it breaks. This is an example of using your intent to extend your ki. If you can develop sensitivity to your ki, then your karate will change as a result.

Japanese characters spelling out "karate."

hara

In traditional Japanese and Chinese medicine, the hara is another name for the abdominal region. By this, we mean the area between the lower ribs and the pelvis.

In terms of karate, the hara is the point through which all movement comes. If you try to kick or punch using only an arm or leg, then your kicks and punches will be weak. If you can connect the movement to your hara, you will use the whole of your body, and the technique will be powerful.

In Japanese thought, the hara is one of the most important energy centers in the human body. Those who are trained to be sensitive to such things can use the hara as a diagnostic area and can deduce physical or emotional problems in a person by touching or examining the hara.

What the therapist is doing is sensing that person's ki. In the hara, all of the different energies in the body meet. By touching this specific area, it is possible to determine the state of those energies.

Your hara is like a second brain. In a way, we already know this: it is in our language, for we have all had a "gut reaction" to a situation.

We all know what it is like when trying to use logic to decide what to do in a certain situation. We may weigh the pros and cons, but then usually decide to go with what our gut instinct told us to do in the first place.

Practicing meditations like the one described later will increase your sense of hara.

If you can develop your sense of hara, you can sidestep considering the pros and cons and go straight for the action. (This is starting to sound like the "just doing it" method of the Zen craftsman. Indeed, a strong hara can be beneficial to the Zen experience.)

In a fighting situation, this means that you will be able to react without having to weigh the process using your conscious mind. This will make you much faster, as well as more accurate—both useful tricks in karate!

chapter 2 is karate for me?

Is karate suitable for you? Well, in short, if you want to do it: yes. The first and most important thing that a karateka must have is the desire to do it. Obviously, this desire will vary from person to person.

You may find that you want to train a lot and eventually become a black belt. Or you may find that a little is enough. In martial arts, the rule is that the more you put into it, the more you get out of it.

So what age range suits karate? Remember when we discussed Gichin Funakoshi? He started his karate training at elementary-school age, the youngest age that children should take up karate. Karate can be an ideal sport for children as it can teach them discipline and self-confidence, backed up by fitness training.

If you are thinking of taking a child to a karate class, speak to the sensei. If the sensei considers your child mature enough for the dojo, then give it a go. Ensure that the sensei understands that children's bodies have not finished growing and that some of the harder stretches and conditioning exercises should therefore be left until they are older. A school will usually also wait for a while before teaching them some of the more dangerous attacking techniques.

No matter what your age, you can have a go at learning karate. If you are worried about your fitness, talk to the sensei and consult your doctor. There are very few medical complaints that will completely exclude you from karate if you have the desire to train. If you, your sensei, and your doctor can together devise a training plan, you should be all right. The more mature student usually finds the concepts of karate easy to grasp, and a karate club can be a great place to meet new friends, too!

There is no reason why men should be better at karate than women. Although some men occasionally try to dominate a sparring session if they are physically stronger than a woman, a sensei will always stop this. In my experience, it is usually the man who loses out if he tries that trick!

what do I need?

When you first enter the dojo or training hall, most teachers will allow you to train in sweatpants and a T-shirt. Karate is usually performed barefoot, which saves on the cost of footwear!

If you then decide that karate is for you, you will be expected to buy a gi. The gi is the traditional outfit worn for training in many martial arts. Karate gis tend to be made from lighter material than judo gis because they are less likely to be torn. The cost of a basic gi usually starts at around $15.

Karate clothes have suffered the same fate as other clothing items: they start low in price, but can become very expensive. There is usually no practical reason why an expensive gi should be better than a cheaper one.

After a while, your sensei will start to teach you kumite, or sparring. If you are to practice free sparring, it is wise to invest in protective equipment. Try to buy the best that you can afford as it will work better and last longer. You can buy all manner of body armor and head gear, some of which are not used by certain karate associations. Your sensei will advise you if you need to buy it. If it is essential, the club will usually have enough supplies.

There are some items that you will need to buy, as outlined on the right.

1	mouthguard	A mouthguard costs a lot less than getting your teeth fixed. Buy one that won't slip out of your mouth.
2	groin protector	I don't need to say much about why a groin protector is advisable! A proper martial-arts groin protector will protect you better than other types. The further it covers your abdominal region without limiting your movement, the better.
3	chest protector	Women will need a chest protector.

belts and grades

When you go to your first karate class, you will see the karate students arranged in neat lines. The ones at the front will probably have black belts, the ones at the back, white belts, while the ones in the middle will be wearing belts of a variety of colors. The colors of the belts are not a fashion statement. They tell you the level of training that the karateka has reached through his or her gradings.

The color of the belts follows a sequence that starts with a white belt and finishes with a black belt. The colors of the belts in between tell you what grade the intermediate karateka has attained.

Each of the belts has to be won in an examination called a grading. This idea was invented by Jigoro Kano, the founder of judo. If you remember your karate history, you'll know that Gichin Funakoshi, the "grandfather of karate," was acquainted with Jigoro Kano. It is therefore not surprising that he adopted the practice, which instantly identifies the more advanced students.

There is a story that after World War II, when Japan was a very poor country, karatekas would dye their belts progressively darker colors until they became black belts.

Nowadays, the many different schools of karate have different colors for their belts. It is important to know the grading system of the school that you are in. In some schools, a blue belt denotes quite an advanced student, for example, while in others, the blue belt is a beginner's belt. On the following page, you will see the traditional colors of the belts, ranging from white to black, in shotokan karate.

There are usually also intermediate grades between the belts, which are denoted by a stripe on the belt.

The word "kyu" means grades away from the black belt (dan). For example, 8th kyu means that the karateka has eight more full gradings to achieve before he or she wins the coveted black belt.

When you reach black-belt level, it does not stop there! Many say that it has just started! There are various levels of black belt, called dan grades. The higher the number, the higher the grade, which is denoted by a stripe on the end of the black belt.

In your grading, you will be required to show the latest kata that you have been learning and possibly some previous ones. Your basic movements, or kihon, will be inspected, and you will have to do some kumite, or sparring.

The mixture and type of each kata, kumite, and kihon will vary, depending on your grade. For example, the beginner is not expected to show any kumite. A black belt, by contrast, will have to show fixed-pattern kumite and free sparring with other black belts.

level	grade	
beginner		white belt
10th kyu		blue belt
9th kyu		red belt
8th kyu		orange belt
7th kyu		orange belt with yellow stripes
6th kyu		yellow belt
5th kyu		green belt
4th kyu		purple belt
3rd kyu		brown belt
2nd kyu		brown belt with white stripes
1st kyu		brown belt with red stripes
1st dan		black belt

the karate class

So much for the theory. Without the practice, it amounts to nothing more than intellectual play. So, you have decided to try karate. What next?

Well, you have two options. You could either try to learn from books like this one and take years to master the techniques in a very limited manner, or you could short-circuit that idea and join a class.

Hopefully, you will opt for the "join a class" option. We will take a look at ways of determining what sort of class you are joining later, but for now, let's consider what happens when you go to a class.

It is normally best to contact the sensei, or teacher, before you go to a class. Although many teachers do not demand that you do this, it gives them a chance to meet you for a few minutes before the class starts. The sensei will normally want to talk to you about any specific needs (medical or non-medical) that you may have. It also gives you the opportunity to get to know your teacher.

What happens next depends on the teacher. Some teachers will ask you to watch for a while so that you can decide whether or not to take the plunge. It is more common these days for the new karate student (karateka) to join in with the beginners. Sometimes a higher-graded student will teach you the basics, such as dojo courtesy (see page 34).

The class will always start with warm-up exercises of some kind. Then the class will usually consist of a mixture of basics (kihon), patterns (kata), and sparring (kumite). The ratio of these will usually vary, depending on the club and what the sensei wants to work on in that lesson. Streching also will normally be inserted at various times during the class.

We will analyze the three physical training areas, kihon, kata, and kumite, throughout this book.

Your sensei will guide you through some warm-up exercises.

types of karate club

We have seen that there are different styles of karate. How do you choose between them? This is a very subjective question. It is like saying which is best, pop music or reggae?

In reality, what most people do is take a look at the nearest club, and if it suits them, they stick with it. This is all right up to a point, but a club's location should not be the only factor in your decision. Have a look at some of the other styles and try to get a flavor of the differences between them. Doing this will improve your overall understanding of karate. Choosing between the styles is really a question of taste. If you like it, then it is good.

Sport karate concentrates on sparring, while traditional karate looks at all aspects of the art.

sport karate or traditional karate?

Within karate, there are two different schools of thought, represented by sports-karate students and traditional karate students.

Most of this book is dedicated to traditional karate because that is my personal preference. In traditional karate, you will cover the whole scope of karate, including basics, kata, sparring, and karate philosophy.

Sports karate is a kind of specialization in which the karateka focuses mainly on the sparring aspect of karate. The students of sports-karate clubs concentrate very hard on their sparring and fitness for sparring. The aim is usually to enter sparring competitions and, hopefully, win them. Sports karate is really a Westernized version of karate that is more competitive than the traditional Japanese karate.

Both traditional karate and sports karate are valid ways of learning karate. Think about what you want from your training, and then make your own decision.

choosing a club

Martial arts are more popular now than they have ever been.

This can be a healthy thing. It means, for example, that potential martial-arts students do not have to stick to the one and only club that is convenient for them to visit regularly. The flip-side of this argument is that quantity does not always equal quality. There are a few very questionable teachers out there!

So you have found a club that is within reasonable traveling distance. The teacher sounds all right on the phone, but how can you tell if it is a good club? Well, the truth is that there is no test that will tell you for certain. It could be that a teacher who has a lot to offer does not meet many of the normal guidelines. Also, what suits one student will not always suit another.

Having said that, there are a few things to look out for. Here is a list of them.

1 **the sensei or teacher** — Is the sensei the type of person whom you feel that you can learn from? Can you speak with the sensei openly? Is the sensei qualified to teach the style?

2 **the senior students** — If you join the club, you will be following what the senior students have done. Is that what you want? Take the opportunity to talk to them, swap a few stories, and get a measure of where they are with their training. Is that what you want to do? Do not forget that much of your teaching in the early days will be from the senior students.

3 **attitude to injury** — Some teachers have a very cavalier attitude to injury. Mention the subject of injury and check that the instructor is saying the kinds of things that you want to hear.

4 **insurance** — Most martial-arts clubs offer some kind of insurance against possible injury. With some of the softer styles, like tai chi, this is not really needed as there is little or no physical contact. In karate, however, you will be sparring and practicing techniques, so it is best to have insurance against injury-causing mistakes.

5 **affiliation** — If an instructor is affiliated to some karate board or body, then he or she will have had to make the grade to become affiliated. This is a good quality benchmark. There is nothing to stop anybody from setting up a martial-arts club. To keep a check on the quality of instruction, many martial-arts associations issue a list of instructors. Your instructor should be on such a list because this will prove that he or she has the necessary skills to teach you the style.

dojo etiquette

Whenever you enter or leave a karate dojo, you should always make a bow, or "rei" (pronounced "ray"). It matters not whether it is a purpose-built dojo or the local village hall: for the purposes of a karate lesson, they are the same. Even if you are just leaving to visit the bathroom, you should always rei on the way out and on the way back in.

At the beginning and end of your class, you will perform either the standing rei or the kneeling rei. When the sensei tells you to split up into pairs for kumite, you should rei to the sensei before breaking away from the group.

You should find your partner quickly and greet him or her with a rei. Before training with your partner, you should rei, and when you have finished training with your partner, you should rei. If you are going to train with another partner, you should do the same again.

So what is all of this bowing for? Many non–martial artists guess that it is similar to shaking hands. This notion probably comes from the habit that Japanese people have of bowing to each other rather than shaking hands. Other people sometimes say that it is kowtowing to the sensei's ego. Both reasons are completely and emphatically wrong!

The rei is a sign of respect. When you enter or leave the dojo, it is a sign that you have respect for the dojo.

When you bow to the sensei, you are not bowing to show subservience to the person standing in front of you. You are bowing to show respect for that person, for what he or she has done in the pursuit of karate knowledge and for all that has gone before him or her.

If you bow to the teachers of the past, you are bowing to the work that they have done and to that which was done before and after them.

When you bow to your training partner, you are showing your partner respect and gratitude for the chance to train with him or her, whoever he or she may be.

With the rei, you should feel a sense of openness and respect. It has nothing at all to do with your ego or that of the person to whom you are bowing. If you subtract the element of respect from martial arts, you are removing one of the most valuable lessons that they have to teach, both to individuals and to the world at large!

There are two sorts of rei that are commonly used in karate, the kneeling rei and the standing rei. Both are very important, so we shall now look at each in turn.

The bow, or "rei," is one of the ways in which a karateka shows respect.

the kneeling rei

The kneeling rei is the most formal version of the rei. It is used at the beginning and end of the class and when bowing to the masters of the past.

1. Start in the attention stance.

2. Move into the ready stance.

3. Bend your right knee. Look ahead.

4. Bend your left knee and kneel down.

5. Drop your weight onto your heels.

6. Place your hands on the floor, thumbs and forefingers touching. Look ahead.

7. Lower your head.

8. Place your right hand on your right thigh.

9. Place your left hand on your left thigh.

To come out of the position, follow these instructions in reverse order.

Note that you will always start by putting your left knee on the floor first. This is because the samurai, who wore their swords on the left, used exactly the same bow. Placing the left knee on the floor first got the weapon out of the way, enabling them to bow.

the standing rei

The standing rei is the rei that is used most frequently. It is also the one that is performed incorrectly the most often! The standing rei is always performed when you need to show courtesy and respect, such as when approaching a new training partner or when leaving or entering the dojo.

1. Start in the ready stance.

2. Place your heels together in the attention stance.

3. Bend forward from the waist, looking ahead.

fitness for karate

If you want to work on your fitness, you will get the best results if you do so frequently. If you are going to practice for two hours a week on top of your classes, it is better for your body if you spread the time over the week rather having a big session at the end of it.

Fitness has many different aspects, depending on how you look at it. It can involve the mind, the body, or even a spiritual connection. The best thing for you to do is to define what you are looking for in exercise. This should change from time to time.

In the beginning, you may find that you get out of breath when practicing your kata. This suggests that you need to work on your cardiovascular training. After overcoming this hurdle, you may need to work on your power or suppleness. Your body will tell you what you require. If you find that you cannot focus your mind when performing your kata, meditation may help. Experiment to see if it does. Make your learning your own!

The exercises that follow are designed so that you can practice them at home. Try to vary your routine. Include other exercises that you may have learned. These exercises are generally quite simple. If you are unsure about anything, ask your instructor because being confused can result in injury. Take it easy, too! Karate is for life. You have all the time that you need, so why rush?

Think about it like this. If you went to the gym and saw a person lift 661 pounds (300 kilograms), you would be impressed, but to try to copy him or her would not be sensible. Unless you were a record-holder, you would injure yourself! The exercises outlined here are similar. If you cannot perform a certain stretch, do not force yourself. Allow your body to change gradually and you will avoid injury. Remember that if you injure yourself by trying to do too much too fast, you will not be able to train!

warm-up exercises

During my years as a practicing martial artist, I have occasionally seen injuries in the training class. During my years of coaching in martial arts, I have also had the chance to speak to fellow coaches about martial arts, and a subject that is often discussed is injuries.

On the whole, karate and other martial arts are surprisingly injury-free. One of the reasons for this is probably that there is a high sense of awareness when practicing the martial arts. If you are in a sparring situation, you will be on your guard against injury, both to yourself and to your partner, for instance.

A common factor associated with many of the injuries that do occur in martial arts is the lack of a proper warm-up. If, for example, you arrive late, it is tempting to run into the dojo, quickly get changed, and start training. If this means that you miss out on your warm-up exercises, you are entering the risk category for injury. For this reason, most instructors force students to perform some warm-up exercises before they are permitted to train.

Another scenario is when you are training at home. It is beneficial to all martial artists to train between lessons. If you do, then you should go through some warm-up exercises, even if they just involve a little stretching.

Put simply, warm-up exercises prepare the body and mind for the exercises to come, and therefore protect you from injury.

By the end of the average karate lesson, you will have started with some gentle warm-up exercises and will probably have moved through some rather intense stretching and cardiovascular exercises. This means that your muscles will have become quite warm during the lesson, making them soft and pliable for stretching. For this reason, it is a good idea to have a cooling-off period after a heavy training session to aid the transition from the training environment to a non-training one.

For the cool-down exercises, your coach will usually take you through some of the warm-up exercises, but will encourage you to perform them in a relatively gentle way.

We will now work through a series of exercises that are useful for warming up your body. These exercises are intended to get your joints moving. The exercises that you need to increase your cardiovascular movement are covered in a separate section.

warm-up exercises: neck movement

If you aren't familiar with the feeling of having a stiff neck, you are lucky! A slight strain in the muscles of the neck can cause headaches, irritability, and sickness. Even worse, it can prevent you from training!

It is useful to include the following neck exercises in your warm-up sequence or just to use them for general body maintenance. Using the exercise when you get up in the morning or during the day can help to avert tension in your neck.

neck exercise 1: left and right

This is probably the simplest exercise that there is! Simplicity is good in warm-up exercises as people are then more likely to do them.

You can be standing or seated. Look straight ahead with your neck centered (1). Do the exercise by turning your head to the left (2) and *gently* stretching your muscles. Hold the stretch for a couple of breaths and return to the center (3) before repeating on the right side (4). Return to the starting position (5).

1.

continued . . .

neck exercise 1: left and right continued

2.

3.

4

5.

1.

neck exercise 2: circling

This is another simple exercise that can be performed seated or standing.

Imagine that you are drawing a large circle with your eyes as you make a circle with your head (1–4). Repeat the exercise in both directions, and remember to keep breathing steadily. Do not let your head rock backward because this may put strain on your upper vertebrae.

2.

3.

4.

warm-up exercises: shoulders

Much of karate has to do with blocks, strikes, and punches from the arms. If your shoulders are as stiff as old pieces of wood, it is impossible for you to perform these actions smoothly.

shoulder exercise 1: rotations

This is a very simple exercise. If you have neck problems, it can be helpful because it can reduce tension in the trapezius muscles in the back of the neck.

1. Inhale as you raise your shoulders in an upward arc.

2. Exhale as you lower your shoulders in a downward arc.

3. Repeat in the other direction.

shoulder exercise 2: windmill

This exercise can be performed quickly or slowly. If you do it slowly, it is good to open the joint. Increasing the speed reduces the ability to open the joint, but helps to get the blood pumping around your shoulder area.

To do the exercise, just swing your arm around in a circle (1–3). Try to perform a similar amount of exercise in both directions with each arm.

variation

For a more challenging exercise, swing one arm forward and one arm backward.

1.   **2.**   **3.**

warm-up exercises: waist

In martial arts, the hips, waist, and abdominal area are the core of your movement. In traditional Japanese shiatsu medicine, the hara (your abdominal region) is your energy center.

If your range of motion in this area is limited, then the whole way that you move your body will also be limited.

Back view.

waist exercise 1: rotation

Try to keep your body straight so that the movement is in your waist and not in your head bobbing up and down. One way of doing this is to focus your eyes on an object. If it looks like the object is moving, then ease off with the exercise until you are within a range of motion when you can keep your head still.

1. Start in a standing position. Put your hands on your kidneys.

2. Push forward with your hands. Rotate your body to the left or right.

3. Repeat in the other direction.

waist exercise 2: rotation

This exercise is fundamental to the way that martial arts work. If you can use your waist area to create a rotation that transmits through the arm, you will have a powerful strike.

Gradually slow down to a stop when you are ready to finish.

1. Start in a standing position. Turn your waist to the left and then to the right, keeping your arms relaxed.

2. As the momentum of your waist increases, your arms will swing out farther. Do not throw your arms out.

warm-up exercises: knees

If you have delicate knees, this exercise is probably best avoided as it is possible that it may
aggravate the condition. If you feel any pain
whatsoever during the exercise, you should
either ease off or stop completely.

knee exercise 1: rotation

You will find that this exercise is
excellent for loosening the hip
joints and also strengthening
the thighs.

When you have finished,
repeat with the other leg.

1. Start by lifting your knee
high in front of your body.

2. Draw a circle with your
knee in one direction. Count
the number of circles that you
do and perform the same
number in the other direction.

knee exercise 2: rotation

In karate, you will be kicking.
Your stance work also
requires that your legs are
strong and supple. These
exercises can help.

1. Put your feet together,
bend your knees, and place
your hands on your knees.

2. Rotate your knees, first in
one direction and then in the
other. Do not overdo the
rotation, though.

warm up-exercises: ankles

Do not forget about your ankles! In stance work, your feet are your connection with the floor. If your ankles are stiff, then the vital connection between your body and the floor is reduced. It is also useful to have supple ankles for kicking.

ankle exercise 1: rotation

This exercise is shown being performed in the standing position, but you can also do it while sitting at a desk. Nobody will see you doing it, and it can have a grounding quality when used in this way.

ankle exercise 2: ankle stretch

Stretch your instep by placing the top of your toes on the floor and gently pushing forward.

1. Touch the floor with the ball of your foot. Make a rotation with your knee. This will work the ankle.

2. Perform the rotation in the other direction. Work with both legs.

stretching for karate

Stretching has many benefits to the karateka. One obvious benefit of warm-up exercises is the reduced risk of injury. The reduction in muscular tension and greater elasticity that stretching brings can reduce the risk of muscular injury or joint sprain.

Stretching has many other benefits, too. The muscular relaxation that comes from stretching causes mental relaxation. This kind of mental relaxation enables a greater body awareness that is vital for the diligent karateka.

Stretching is only of benefit when done properly, however. Karateka must incorporate stretching into their daily routines if they want to achieve proper results. Stretches must be performed slowly and gradually.

Getting a training partner to push your legs into a long stretch once a week is an inadvisable method that can lead to long-term injuries.

There are various approaches to stretching. Science has had a lot to say about the human body, and this has led to ideas that have replaced the need for painful exercises that can damage your body. Some commonly used stretching methods are outlined here.

ballistic and dynamic stretching

In ballistic stretching, you bounce into the stretch. This is a rather dangerous method because it does not give the muscle tissues time to adapt to the stretch, although it can be effective for increasing your range of motion.

In ballistic and dynamic stretching, you attempt to move into the stretch and thereby increase your range of motion. When you feel the stretch reach its maximum, you ease off before waiting for the muscles to adjust. Then you can go into the stretch again. A lunge stretch is demonstrated above.

static stretching

Simple and safe, static stretching involves stretching to your furthest point and holding. It must be balanced with power training to maintain muscle performance. This is a side split.

passive stretching

In passive stretching, you try to relax your body while an external force extends the stretch. A common example of this is when one karateka helps the other to stretch his or her legs by pushing them out.

Passive stretching is effective, but can lead to muscular soreness.

1. Sit opposite your partner, with your feet touching your partner's ankles.

2. Grab each other's belts.

3. Both of you should now pull to bring your bodies closer and increase the stretch.

4. Your partner should now hold your elbows.

5. Lean back *slowly* to increase the stretch for your partner.

active stretching

There are two types of active stretching. The first is when you try to hold a fixed position that causes your body to stretch, such as the leg raise shown below.

The other type of active stretching is when you use your muscles to push against a force, such as somebody holding your leg. After the muscular exertion, you should try to lift your leg to a higher position.

stretch for the feet

This stretch is especially useful in helping you to learn how to curl back your toes for the front and roundhouse kicks.

1. Kneel on all fours, with your toes underneath you. Keep your back straight.

2. Exhale as you force your buttocks backward and downward. You should feel the stretch in the soles of your feet.

stretch for the lower leg

This stretch is particularly useful for the lower leg and Achilles tendon. It can also help to reduce the possibility of a cramp occurring in the lower leg.

1. Bend your body over and support your weight with your arms. Increase the stretch by moving your hands closer to your feet.

2. The foot with its heel down is the one being stretched. You can either stretch both at the same time by having both heels down or one at a time by alternating feet.

stretch for the hamstrings

This stretch for the hamstrings is also a useful exercise for opening up the groin area. It is incorporated into most martial-arts stretching routines.

1. Squat on the floor, with your weight being supported by the leg that is flexed. You can stabilize the posture by grabbing your ankles.

2. Exhale as you lower your upper torso toward the leg being stretched. You should feel the stretch in the back of your leg.

stretch for the adductors

Strong and supple adductor muscles are essential for side kicks.

Squat with your feet flat on the floor and toes turned slightly outward. Place your elbows on your thighs. When you exhale, use your elbows to push your thighs out.

stretch for quadriceps

It is impossible to kick without using the quadriceps. This will help you to keep them looser.

1. Lie face down on the floor and then grab an ankle.

2. As you exhale, pull your ankle toward your buttock. If your knee feels uncomfortable, stop the exercise.

stretch for hips and gluteals

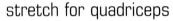

Keep your hips supple to avoid hip pain in later life.

1. Lie on your back, with your arms stretched out. Extend your leg.

2. Exhale as you lower your foot to your opposite hand. Keep your entire upper trunk and elbows flat on the floor. If your shoulder starts to lift, decrease the range.

stretch for lower torso

This stretch is part of many yoga routines, and is sometimes called the cobra.

1. Lie face downward on the floor.

2. Put your palms next to your waist, with your fingers pointing up the length of your body.

3. Simultaneously exhale and push down with your hands. Arch your back while contracting your buttocks.

stretch for upper back

It is quite difficult to stretch the muscles in the upper back. Try this exercise.

1. Interlace your fingers and make your back rounded as shown.

2. Exhale and push your hands forward and back with the muscles in your upper back.

stretch for pectorals

For this exercise, it is best if you sit on a chair. If a chair is not available, you can still perform the exercise, but it will not be as strong.

1. Sit down and interlock your hands behind your head. The top of the chair should be at mid-chest level.

2. Push back your upper torso and also push your elbows backward.

stretch for shoulders

Some flexible people find this exercise surprisingly difficult. If you are one of them, treat it as you would any other exercise and work on it gradually. According to the yoga guru B. K. S. Iyengar, it is the difficult exercises that benefit our bodies the most.

1. Start with your hands behind your back.

2. Exhale and push your fingers upward.

stretch for arms and wrists

Be attentive when it comes to arm and wrist stretches. Most of them can double up as arm and wrist locks if you apply them to another person. This is one such example.

1. Extend your left arm.

2. Put your right arm under the elbow of your left arm.

3. Bring your left hand back so that your right hand can grab your left hand or wrist.

4. Exhale as you press lightly downward with your right hand.

cardiovascular exercises

If you ever enter a sparring tournament, you will instantly understand why the karateka must have a high level of cardiovascular fitness. Although the bout may only be three minutes long, most people finish it with hardly a breath left in their lungs.

If you have found this, then you are in good company! Bruce Lee said that a major turning point in his training program was after just such an experience. He was in a fight against several other people. He won, but was surprised how much it took out of him.

So even the greatest martial artists need to work on their cardiovascular fitness. In short, it is going to cost you a lot of sweat if you want to be really fit! But what is the best way of working on it?

The answer is to train as frequently as possible. Cross-training is an excellent way of boosting your fitness. You may not be able to go to the dojo every night, but there is nothing stopping you from running, swimming, cycling, or whatever you enjoy. The key lies in your enjoyment.

I do not like running, but do enjoy swimming. This means that I emphasize the swimming more than the running. However, running is very good exercise, so it is advisable to do a bit every now and then, as your needs dictate.

As a supplement to whatever cardiovascular training you enjoy, you will need to build more into your practice routine at home. Your sensei will give you a set of exercises to do in your warm-up sessions to get your muscles warm. If you are practicing at home, you should really

include some, or all, of the following exercises to get your heart beating faster.

The exercises have been specifically picked to work with other aspects of your fitness that you will need for karate training, such as coordination, reflexes, and suppleness.

cardio exercise 1:
star jumps

If you need to warm up quickly, a couple of hundred star jumps will do the trick. Try to stay light on your feet: this exercise should not make the furniture rattle too much.

To get the most from the exercise, make sure that your hands touch at the highest point of the jump.

1. Start in the attention stance.

2. Jump up and spread your legs as your hands travel upward. Jump back into the attention position.

cardio exercise 2:
running in place

Note that running in place is not intended to replace proper running. Try the following routine.

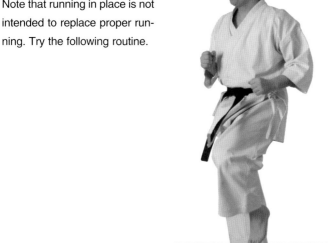

1	1 minute of normal running
2	30 seconds of running as fast as you can
3	30 seconds of normal running
4	30 seconds of running as fast as you can

You can continue in this manner for as long as you want.

cardio exercise 3:
spin jump

This is definitely an exercise that you should not do if you live in an apartment building, unless you want your neighbors banging on the ceiling!

Bend your knees. Jump as high as you can and spin through a complete circle.

cardio exercise 4:
tuck jump

This exercise helps you to build up the explosive power in your legs that is vital for powerful kicking.

Bend your knees. Jump as high as you can, but try to tuck yourself into a ball at the top of the jump. The movement is similar to cannonballing into a swimming pool.

cardio exercise 5: stretch jump

This exercise is the same as exercise 4, except that you expand rather than contract.

Start from a standing position. Jump as high as you can and reach upward with your arms as you jump.

cardio exercise 6: "cycling"

This exercise is very similar to the concept of running in place.

Lie on your back and pretend that you are pedaling a bicycle. The technique that makes it effective is using short "sprint" periods like you did in the running-in-place exercise (cardio exercise 2).

cardio exercise 7: "speed ball"

This exercise is excellent for improving your upper-body strength, as well as your aerobic capacity. All that you are doing here is pretending that you are using the sort of speed ball that boxers use. If you actually have a speed ball to train with, even better.

Use the technique of going slow and sprinting as you did for running in place (exercise 2).

cardio exercise 8: repetitive punching

This is a classic karate exercise. All you need to do is keep punching.

Try to keep an even rhythm in the beginning. When you have become looser, try sequences of punching quickly and punching slowly like you used for running in place (exercise 2).

strength training for karate

If you look at most professional martial artists, you will normally see a well-developed physique. The top people in similar activities, such as boxing and kickboxing, also look as though they are in tip-top condition.

In modern times, this almost invariably means that the person has been doing some kind of working out or strength training. In the old days, it was thought that too much gym work would make a person muscle-bound and slow. As long as you follow a sensible training routine, the opposite is more likely to happen, however.

Enhanced muscle capability brings more advantages, such as greater power and improved physical stamina, as long as it is coupled with stretching and cardiovascular work.

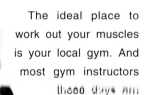

The ideal place to work out your muscles is your local gym. And most gym instructors those days are

more than capable of devising a training program that is suitable for your needs as a karateka.

It may be that you do not live near a gym, however, or cannot attend one for some other reason, such as time or financial constraints. This need not be a barrier to your training.

If you want to buy some equipment to use at home, a Swiss ball is ideal. The Swiss ball was originally used for people who were in rehabilitation from various injuries. It is basically a large elastic rubber beach ball that you do exercises on. And, very importantly, it is cheap!

The advantage of the Swiss ball is that it forces you to use your stabilizing, or core, muscles. As the name "core" suggests, these muscles are the ones that are deeper inside your body than the exterior sets. If you can improve the quality of your core muscles, you will improve your balance and strength.

I know a rugby coach who started using the Swiss ball with a professional team. The results for the team were greater strength, balance, and coordination on the rugby field. Strength, balance, and coordination are also pretty useful in the dojo!

The following exercises introduce you to useful techniques for building up your strength at home. Where suitable, I have also shown how to incorporate Swiss-ball training into your routine. An important part of strength training is keeping it varied. Your body responds well to variety. So try different combinations of exercises. Be creative!

strength exercise 1: the push-up

The push-up is an old favorite in most fitness routines. It is a simple exercise that works very well. It is also a good indicator of your upper-body strength. Good upper-body strength and arm movements can help you to move the whole of your body more fluidly.

There are many versions of the push-up, such as one-armed, on hands, and on knuckles. We will look at the basic push-up, as well as a few other suggestions. Remember to keep your back straight.

1. Lie on the floor, with your hands on the floor beside your shoulders.

2. Straighten your arms to push up your body. Then lower your body by bending your elbows until your chest is close to the floor. This is a complete push-up.

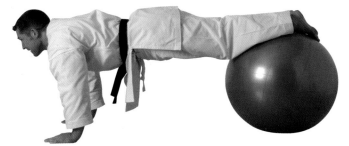

variations

1	If you find the push-up difficult, try push-ups from the knees.
2	If the push-up is very easy, try raising your feet (put them on a solid box or a step). The higher your feet, the more difficult the push-up.

swiss-ball variations

1	Try doing the push-up with your hands on a Swiss ball. (You will find this more difficult than it sounds.)
2	If you have well-developed upper-body strength, try putting your feet on a Swiss ball and doing the push-up.

strength exercise 2: the sit-up

Strong abdominal muscles are the center of your movement in martial arts. If your abdominal muscles are weak, it is more difficult for your back to support your weight and the result can be bad posture.

If your posture is bad, then your center of gravity will rise, and it will be more difficult for you to balance your body. Poor balance means that it is more difficult to generate power in your punches and kicks.

The variation of the sit-up described here is sometimes called the crunch.

1. Lie on the floor, with your back flat and your knees raised. Cross your arms in front of your chest.

2. Lift your shoulders from the floor. Keep your arms crossed, but do not clench the muscles. This is one sit-up.

variations

These are some variations that you may wish to try.

1	**Work your oblique muscles by pushing your left shoulder toward your right knee and vice versa.**
2	**Work higher in the abdomen by raising your knees and buttocks for the exercise.**

swiss-ball variation

I ean back on the Swiss ball and perform the sit-up in the same way. Your hands should be near your head, but not making contact with it. Do not overextend your back by leaning back too far.

strength exercise 3: the plank

This exercise is called the plank because your body should be as straight as a plank when you perform it. It is excellent for working your abdominal and back muscles.

Lie on the floor on your abdomen. Tuck your hands under your body in a "praying" position. Touch the floor with the balls of your feet. Lift your body with your abdominal muscles and hold it there. Keep your back straight. Keep your breathing steady and even.

swiss-ball variation

This is an excellent exercise for the Swiss ball. Perform exactly the same exercise, but rest your elbows and forearms on the Swiss ball. It is easier if you link your hands because the structure is then more stable. When you are accustomed to the exercise, you will no longer need to link your hands.

A variation from the side can also be performed on the Swiss ball. This will really test your balance!

strength exercise 4: reverse plank

The reverse-plank exercise works in much the same way as the plank exercise (exercise 3), except the other way around. This reversal of position means that the back muscles are emphasized more than the abdominal muscles, although both are used.

Lie on your back, with your arms by your sides and your knees bent. Tuck in your feet so that they are fairly close to your buttocks.

Use your legs and abdominal muscles to lift your body. Keep your back straight by clenching your buttocks.

variation

If you like this exercise, you can extend it into the yogic exercise called the "bridge" by placing your hands behind your shoulders and lifting the upper part of your body.

swiss-ball variation

When doing this exercise with a Swiss ball, you are effectively doing the "bridge" exercise with the ball to support your upper-middle back. Once the exercise has become easy, you can increase the pressure by placing a heavy book or small weight on your abdominal area.

strength exercise 5: grip

When you make a fist, it is not just the muscles in your hands that are involved. If you clench your fist tightly now, you will be able to feel all of the muscles in your forearms contracting.

The stronger these muscles in your hands and forearms are, the tighter you will be able to contract your fist for the moment of impact. In karate, your fist is tightly clenched to make the impact stronger.

The following exercise is good for working these muscles. It also has an added benefit. In traditional Chinese and Japanese medicine, there is a whole collection of energy channels or meridians that finish in the fingers. This exercise helps you to "pump" the meridians and enhance the flow of energy in a positive way.

Hold out your hands in front of your body. Clench your fists. Then unclench your fists. Repeat ten times. Repeat, holding your hands by your sides. Repeat, holding your hands high. Repeat, holding your hands behind your body.

Increase the repetitions as your muscles become accustomed to the exercise.

variation

There are as many energy meridians and muscles in the feet as in the hands. Try sitting with your legs stretched out and then perform the same exercise with your toes. You could probably get away with doing this exercise while sitting at your desk!

strength exercise 6: horse-riding stance

I was once told by a senior martial-arts instructor, somewhat in jest, that if you can manage to stand in a wide horse-riding stance for half an hour a day for a year, then you will be a champion. Looking back on the comment, it probably held a grain of truth. If you have the mental and physical determination to perform the exercise that much on top of your normal training, you deserve something!

The exercise will increase the power in your legs and improve your balance. It will also improve your mental and physical stamina.

To perform the exercise, you will need to quieten your mind. If your mind is too busy, you will be mentally trying to move on to the next exercise. It is therefore truly a martial-arts exercise!

Start with your feet approximately one shoulder-width apart and the inner edges of your feet parallel. Bend your knees and tuck under your sacrum (part of your vertebrae) as though your buttocks were resting on the edge of a chair. Now extend your hands to counterbalance your weight.

To start with, most people find this position quite difficult to hold for more than a minute or two. However, that is the easy part! When you can hold the position for around five to ten minutes, there are three things that you can do to make the exercise harder.

1	**Make your stance wider. There is no need to go over the top when doing this. One-and-a-half to two shoulder-widths should be enough.**
2	**Make your stance lower. At the lowest point, your thighs should be parallel to the floor.**
3	**Try a combination of the two to make a stance that is both lower and wider. It is easier to get into the lower stance if your feet are in a wider position.**

Your arms do not have to be in the position shown here. If you want, there is nothing stopping you from practicing a few blocks, punches, and strikes while in this position. It may even take your mind off how your legs are feeling!

The important thing with this exercise, as with any other, is not to overdo it or strain your body. Keep your back straight while training and gradually build up your strength.

meditation

I have discussed what they think the main differences are between training in the West and training in the East with many martial artists from Japan, Korea, and China. One of the most common things mentioned is meditation.

In the West, we all too often do not make time for meditation, and therefore lose out on its benefits. Among the many benefits of meditation are a reduction in stress (thereby helping the immune system) and increased clarity of thought.

Now, clarity of thought is a pretty useful thing in karate. Imagine that you are trying to break something with your punch. Do you think that you can manage it if your mind is wandering? The same applies to kata and sparring. If you cannot focus your mind, you will sooner or later reach a point beyond which you cannot progress.

Meditation is like weight lifting for the mind. In the beginning, sitting there trying to do and think nothing may feel odd, and even pointless until you have experienced the results.

If you can only manage to meditate for a few minutes a day, then so be it! You can work on it in the same way that you would on anything else, namely gradually. If you find meditation difficult in the beginning, this may indicate that it is what your mind and body need. Great fruits will be reaped!

There are many methods of meditation, including practicing karate. We will now take a look at a very simple, but effective, meditation method called breathing into the hara.

breathing into the hara

Your hara is your energy center. Focusing your breathing into that area is useful for calming your energy. You may find this technique especially useful if your daily routine forces you to train at night. It will help you to calm your body and mind and aids restful sleep.

1 Assume the kneeling position shown here, with your hands resting gently on your thighs. If this makes your knees feel uncomfortable, try sitting on cushions or cross-legged. The kneeling position gives you a firm base on which to support your back and keep it straight.

2 Close your eyes and listen to your breathing. Is it fast, slow, regular, irregular, deep, or shallow? Do not judge, just notice.

3 Now rest your hands on your abdomen. When you breathe in and out, do your hands move?

4 Gently try to adjust your breathing rhythm so that your hands move outward when you inhale and inward when you exhale. You are now doing abdominal breathing, a popular technique in martial arts and yoga.

5 Carry on with the abdominal breathing for a few deep breaths. Feel the air going deep into your lungs. Imagine that you are breathing air down into your abdomen.

6 After a few good, deep breaths to clear your lungs, breathe more gently. Try to make your breathing as smooth and deep as you can. This should be a very gentle stage of the meditation. Imagine that the point under your hands is becoming denser as you breathe into it.

7 Try to make your breathing silent, but deep. Continue visualizing bringing energy into your hara.

8 When you have had enough, gently bring yourself out of the meditation. Shake out your body to bring it back to life again and to distribute the ki.

chapter 4 stances and stepping in karate

One of the most important aspects of martial-arts training, whether it is in karate or any other style, is footwork. If your footwork is not good, then you need to work on it. No successful martial artist ever considered footwork to be unimportant.

Imagine, for a moment, a cannon on board a ship or defending the ramparts of a castle. When a cannonball is fired, there is a reaction from the explosion in the gunpowder. This reaction causes the cannonball to shoot out, but also forces the cannon to move backward if it is not securely fixed into place.

This is one of the principles upon which karate stances are based. If you fire out your fist like a cannonball, you have released a good punch. But if your feet slip back, some energy is wasted. This is not good because part of what you are trying to achieve in karate is focusing all of your energy into a single point.

Now imagine that you actually hit something. This time, the reaction will be even stronger because the impact reflects backward through your body as a reaction force. If the reaction

force knocks you off balance or throws you back, you will probably be in worse trouble than you were before the punch!

The solution to this is to use a good, strong stance ("dachi" in Japanese) that can withstand the impact of the reaction to your techniques. The stances in karate are similar to those in most martial arts. For example, the front stance in karate is also used in other Japanese arts, such as judo and aikido. Chinese and Korean styles tend toward slightly shorter stances, for reasons of their own, although this is not a hard-and-fast rule.

The next thing to be concerned with after your stance is how to move in that stance. If you are rooted to the spot, you will not be much of a martial artist! When stepping, the physics are designed to try to maintain the integrity of the stance. This means that you should be well balanced when making transitions between your stances.

Your stepping and stances are also the key to your distancing. If you are good with your footwork, it is possible to throw a person off balance just by stepping toward them in the correct way. Clearly, correct footwork is an aspect of the art that will be refined throughout your progress in karate. How you understand your footwork in a year's time should be different to your current comprehension.

natural stance: hachiji dachi

The natural stance is the one that you use at the beginning of all of the katas and other formal exercises. The stance is sometimes called the "yoi" stance for that reason.

Your body should be straight and well aligned. This shows that you have strong spirit. Stay alert when in the stance. If you allow your mind to drift when in the stance before performing your kata at a grading, for example, your instructor will notice. You will have made your first mistake before actually doing anything. Karate is as much about your state of mind as your body!

The natural stance is a neutral stance that is neither aggressive nor retreating. Your feet should be a hip-width apart.

The instructions to the right tell you how to get into the natural stance from the attention stance (heisoku dachi).

1	Stand at attention, with your arms by your sides.
2	Cross your forearms.
3	Step forward with your right foot as you uncross your arms.

front stance: zenkutsu dachi

The front stance is a strong attacking stance that can also be used for blocks. The power of the stance is in pushing your energy and strength forward, hence its obvious application for attacking. It can also be used to make a retreat. If you are in a situation where you need to retreat, but also display strength, you can step backwards in the front stance.

Your weight should be split approximately 70/30 between your legs, with 70 percent on your front leg. The stance should be the width of your shoulders and one-and-a-half shoulder-widths in length. Your front leg should be bent at the knee and your back leg should be straight. Your hips should face forward. Both feet should stay flat on the floor. Your rear foot should be at an angle of around 45 degrees.

Side view.

The front stance is probably the most common stance in karate. Try to program your body so that you automatically step into it correctly.

stepping in the front stance

1. Start in the natural stance (hachiji dachi).

2. Move your right leg forward and bend your knee. As you push forward from your left heel, allow your left foot to turn through an angle. Keep your right leg bent as you bring your left foot close to your right. At this moment, your weight should stay on your right leg. Try to keep your balance so that you do not wobble.

3. Step forward with your left foot into the next front stance.

To continue stepping, just follow this sequence.

If you want to step backward in the back stance, the procedure is exactly the same. Just follow the instructions in reverse.

back stance: kokutsu dachi

As you can probably work out from your newly gleaned knowledge of the front stance, the back stance is primarily a defensive stance that can also be used for attacking.

In this stance, the weight split is still 70/30, but in reverse. Your back leg carries most of the weight. Your heels should be in line with each other. Again, the front foot is straight and the back foot is positioned at an angle.

This stance can be quite demanding for the standing leg because all of the muscles are compressed in that leg. As you start to tire, be careful that you do not lean forward and put too much weight on your front leg or allow your knee to collapse. Remember your karate spirit! After training, your muscles will become accustomed to the stance and it will not feel difficult.

getting into the back stance

Follow the steps illustrated below to get into the back stance.

1. Start in the attention stance.

2. Turn your right foot to an angle of 45 degrees and move your left leg forward.

3. Lower your weight onto your right leg and place your left heel on the floor.

straddle-leg stance: kiba dachi

The straddle-leg stance is sometimes called the horse or horse-riding stance. The idea is that you should look like you are riding a horse, which doesn't just mean having your legs apart. In horse riding, if you are on the flat, it is good to keep your back straight. And in this stance, it is essential that you keep your back straight.

The inner edges of your feet should be parallel and about two shoulder-widths apart. You need to sink down on to your knees, so your knees will be turned outward slightly. Your weight should be equally distributed between your feet.

This stance is very useful for sideways attacks, such as the side-snapping kick. It can also be used as a stable base for a front attack if you want to deliver a powerful punch.

The straddle-leg stance can be very difficult for beginners because it is demanding on the muscles. Try standing in the posture for a few minutes a day to build up your strength.

cat stance: neko ashi dachi

The cat stance is so called because it is said to resemble the way that a cat steps. A cat will touch the floor with its foot before putting weight on

it. In the cat stance, all of your weight is on the rear, standing leg, while the ball of the leading foot gently touches the floor.

It is a difficult stance to hold, but has a certain kind of elegance. For this reason, it is not included in most of the katas that a beginner will be expected to perform. However, you may be asked to show that you know the stance, so do not disregard it, even if you are a beginner.

The main usage for this stance is when you suddenly need to move your body backward in a defensive posture. If you step back into the cat stance, your front leg is in an ideal position to deliver a front kick.

It is not usually a stance that is used for stepping in kata or kumite, although some clubs may encourage stepping in the cat stance to train the legs.

The cat stance is usually used as a defensive or retreating stance.

chapter 5 **basic techniques**

As with any skill or art form, there are certain basic techniques that you must understand before you learn the intricacies. With karate, they are the hand and foot techniques.

Generally speaking, these techniques are used either to strike or to evade a strike. When your understanding becomes deeper, you will begin to see that blocks can be used as strikes and vice versa. Some of the basic techniques also have applications as locks and throws.

For now, we will look at a single application for each technique. Always try to think of new applications for your techniques, though. This will help you to make your karate your own and to learn very effectively.

If you want to improve your karate, work on your basic techniques. It is of little use knowing many different kata, but still not being able to punch your way out of a paper bag! If your technique is good, you can apply it to your kata, your sparring, and everything else. Basic techniques are the building blocks of karate.

Improving one technique will have a positive effect on all of your other techniques. So start by learning one technique at a time, such as the lower block.

Practice the lower block, or whichever technique you have chosen to focus on, at home for five to ten minutes each day. Keep working on the same movement for six to eight weeks before moving on to the next one, for example, the punch.

making a fist

Making a fist is probably one of the most basic of all human reactions. If you are on a roller-coaster ride, when the carriage suddenly shoots down one of the slopes, the chances are that you will make a fist. The chances also are that that fist is correct.

When you overanalyze things, they can sometimes become mixed up. If you are working from a pure gut reaction, as you are when the roller coaster is speeding downward, your mind will not confuse matters by getting in the way.

Although it is true that some styles, especially the Chinese styles, use specialized fists with a protruding knuckle, these are not within the scope of this basic karate book.

1. Open your hand.

2. Bend your fingers.

3. Luck your fingers tightly into your palm.

4. Tightly fold your thumb over your fingers. Remember to keep your thumb tightly tucked out of the way as it is easy to catch and break it when sparring.

The strike area is the two front knuckles. Your two front knuckles and forearm should be in alignment.

kimae: the art of breath control

Kimae is the ability to synchronize your breathing with your technique. On a basic level, this means that you exhale for outward-going movements and inhale when the movement is coming back to you.

Consider the punch, for example. Without trying to control them, let a few punches out and take note of your breathing. Most people find that when they punch, they exhale. This makes it obvious that they inhale between punches when they pull their fist back ready to strike again.

So far it's not rocket science! If you can co-ordinate your breathing with your movements, you will have a connection between the external part of the movement, that is, the punch, and the internal part, the breathing.

Now we come to our first difficulty: trying too hard. From the beginning, your breathing should be entirely natural, and not forced. People who worry too much about breathing in the early days of practice normally find themselves in all sorts of confusion. A karateka performing the whole of the taikyoku shodan without breathing would not be the first, or last, to do so!

But there is more to kimae than just this. When you have been practicing for a while, and your mind has learned to let your body take over, there is a next level.

A famous legend in martial arts concerns the "one-inch punch" performed by Bruce Lee. Many people think that because Bruce Lee was respon-sible for the punch, it belongs exclusively to the Chinese styles.

The first thing to ask is, how did he do it? Imagine that you could perform kimae to an advanced level. This would mean that you would be able to focus all of your breath and power into a short distance. The advanced karateka does this all of the time at the end of a punch.

What happens is that very close to the end of the punch, all of the muscles become momen-tarily tense and the breath is forced out in a short burst. Another effect of this is that the mind becomes wonderfully focused on the tech-nique that you are performing. In short, kimae is the combination of body movement, breath control, and intent of the mind, all in one short burst.

You should try to perform kimae at the end of every block, strike, punch, or kick in your karate. This short burst of breath can often make karatekas produce an audible noise as the air blasts through their lungs. This brings us nicely to the next subject: kiai.

kiai

If you stand outside a karate class, unless the walls have been soundproofed, you will usually hear a lot of shouting. This is not just because the karateka are having fun. What is happening is that they are using a technique called kiai. Many martial arts use this technique, although some call it by a different name.

So why do they do it? Well, if you have just read about kimae, you will be thinking along the right lines. If you shout when performing a technique, it forces all of the air out of your lungs and constricts the abdomen. Both are essential ingredients of kimae.

But there is another reason for using kiai. If you are on the attack and simultaneously yell, then it can nearly frighten your opponent out of his or her skin! As you are in a fighting situation, you need all of the advantages that you can get. If all that it takes to gain half a second is a good, loud shout, then it is worth trying. In half a second, you can deliver a knockout blow!

Kiai is an expression of your karate spirit.

striking areas

If you go into a martial-arts store, the chances are that you will see some kind of poster that shows you all of the "vital points" that you need for karate. These points are usually at acupuncture points called "tsubos." Frequently, a tsubo will also be on a point that common sense tells you to protect, such as an ear or eye.

The importance of these vital points is that they are targets at which to aim your strikes. The poster will often also give a description of the best way to hit a vital point. These charts are generally for the highly advanced student.

There are hundreds of vital points around the head and neck. If you get a good strike to the area with something like a reverse knife-hand strike, it matters very little which point you have hit.

If your technique is good and your intention powerful, it matters very little where you hit your opponent, but rather how you hit him or her. This is a more advanced karate concept.

There is no attempt to describe the techniques to use for an area. This is that when people move. If a person is facing you straight on, you need a hooking punch to hit the side of the head. If he or she turns, you can do it with a simple jab.

punching

Everybody knows how to punch. Well, that is what a lot of people think. You just clench your fist and let it rip! But along with that instinctive knowledge, we also know that some people are better at punching than others.

In karate, the mechanics of the punch are examined in fine detail. We find that what starts out as a basic movement that everybody has a concept of is refined to a high level. Which part of the hand do you punch with? Where do you punch? Where does the power come from? What range does the punch have?

These are questions that karateka must be able to answer about their punches (zuki). But remember that no amount of understanding and intellectual analysis can replace practice!

Remember these points about punching.

1	**Punches travel in straight lines in karate.**
2	**There should always be a reaction hand with a punch, that is, you pull one hand back as you punch with the other.**
3	**You should exhale on the punch.**
4	**There is usually a twist at the end of the punch.**
5	**Timing is crucial.**

The basic punch is the straight punch, or choku zuki, as described on the following pages. Understand this punch before moving on to learn others.

The punch is one of the basic karate techniques.

straight punch:
choku zuki

1	Contact area	two front knuckles
2	Range	medium to long
3	Target area	anywhere!
4	Power	strong
5	Speed	medium to fast
6	Difficulty level	easy
7	Suitability for sparring	good

The straight punch is the basic building block of many of the other punches. It is fairly fast, and has the power to stop an opponent. It is versatile, and can be used on any target.

The most difficult parts of this punch are timing, or coordinating the left hand with the right hand (both should move at the same speed), and achieving the twist at the end of the punch.

The straight-punch application.

Because it is so fundamental to the karate style, it should always be practiced.

The punch is shown being performed in the horse-riding stance. If it were done in the front stance, it would become another punch. It could also be executed in the back stance.

Try practicing the movement slowly to learn how to coordinate your hands, and gradually build up the speed. The more advanced karateka can perform dynamic tensioning.

1. Start in the horse-riding stance, with your left fist held out, and your right fist by your belt.

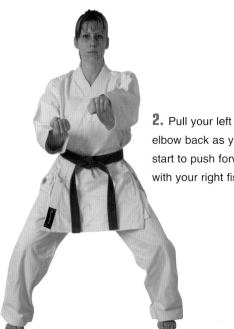

2. Pull your left elbow back as you start to push forward with your right fist.

3. Continue moving your elbow and fist. Both fists should stop moving at the same time, when your wrist twists.

stepping punch: oi zuki

1	**Contact area**	two front knuckles
2	**Range**	long
3	**Target area**	frequently mid-section, but can be used anywhere
4		very strong: it has the weight of your body behind it
5	**Speed**	medium
6	**Difficulty level**	easy, but requires coordination of the arms and legs
7	**Suitability for sparring**	good

If you step forward into the front stance while executing a straight punch, you will have performed a stepping punch. This can be used when you need to get closer to an opponent in order to hit him or her.

It is very a powerful punch because it concentrates the whole of your body weight into a very small striking area. It is not as fast as the choku zuki (straight) punch because you need to step to perform the punch.

As with all punches, timing is the key to max-imizing its power!

Stepping-punch application.

1. Start in the left front stance, with your left arm in the position for a low block.

2. Raise your left arm as you step up.

3. Step forward with your right leg into the right front stance.

4. Twist your body and pull back your left arm as you punch with your right fist.

reverse punch:
gyaku zuki

1	**Contact area**	two front knuckles
2	**Range**	medium to long
3	**Target area**	middle section or high section
4	**Power**	very strong: it is usually the strongest punch
5	**Speed**	medium to fast
6	**Difficulty level**	easy, but power must come from the waist
7	**Suitability for sparring**	good

If you have ever been to a karate display where the karateka and sensei were showing their power by breaking slabs of wood with a punch, it is highly likely that they were using the reverse punch.

The reverse punch is relatively simple to learn and *very* powerful. The key to this punch is the same as that for all of the others: co-ordinating it with the movement of your waist backed up by the use of your reaction arm.

Remember that extra power is available to you if you time your exhalation to coincide with the outward movement of the punch.

Reverse-punch application.

A common mistake is to overextend yourself. This always means that you will lose coordination of your body. If your heel lifts from the floor as shown on the right, you are overextending. This applies to all movements. Overextension reduces your power.

This punch is normally executed in a fixed front stance. It is possible to step forward and do it or to do it in the back stance, as in the heian katas.

The punch finishes as you twist your hips into the final position. The movement of both fists should finish simultaneously with the twist. Your right fist twists as you exhale at the last moment.

The reverse punch is so called because the opposite arm and leg are pushed forward, that is, if your left leg is pushed forward, your right fist is extended and vice versa. The same logic

The heel is lifting here, which is a common mistake.

applies to such techniques as reverse-knife hand. If your punching arm is on the same side of your body as your forward leg, that is, both are on the left or right, it is the forward punch.

1. Start in the left front stance, with your left arm extended.

2. Pull back your left elbow as you start to punch with your right fist. Continue pulling back with your left elbow as you push the punch forward.

jabbing punch: kizami zuki

1	**Contact area**	ideally, two front knuckles, but the whole of the front fist is common in sparring
2	**Range**	short to medium
3	**Target area**	head
4	**Power**	the least powerful, but it can still have quite a sting!
5	**Speed**	medium to fast
6	**Difficulty level**	easy, but power must come from the waist
7	**Suitability for sparring**	good (most common sparring punch)

Every boxer needs to develop a good jab. This is not because you will normally score a knock-out blow with a jab, although it has happened. It is because a good, fast, powerful jab opens the way for a more powerful technique.

Some tournament fighters are very keen on the jab-jab-punch rhythm. In this, the two leading jabs are used to open the defenses and the final punch is when he or she gets to score, so watch out for it!

Jabbing-punch application.

The essence of the karate jab is the same as a boxer's. Watch and learn from the boxers on television as they are normally masters of it.

The jab is a very simple punch that is performed by extending the arm. Do not forget to rotate your waist, for there is hardly any power in the jab unless you do so.

1. Start by assuming a sparring stance.

2. Drive out the punch by twisting your waist.

3. Now snap your arm back into its original position.

hooking punch: kage zuki

1	**Contact area**	ideally, two front knuckles, but the whole of the front fist is common in sparring
2	**Range**	short
3	**Target area**	the head; sometimes used for the middle section
4	**Power**	medium
5	**Speed**	slow to medium
6	**Difficulty level**	easy; requires coordination with the reaction hand
7	**Suitability for sparring**	good

The hooking punch is another technique that boxers use in their sport. It is also the most common punch for people who have not trained in a martial style to use. If you are unfortunate enough to have seen a fight in real life, the chances are that there was very little real technique involved, and that the punch that you saw was the hooking punch.

It is less common in martial arts because it is relatively easy to block. One of the reasons for this is that it travels in a semicircle. Most karate

Hooking-punch application.

punches travel in a straight line, the shortest way to get between two points. This can mean that the fighter who is limited to hooking punches alone will not be as fast as the one who can perform straight punches, and that the straight punch will get through.

This all makes the hooking punch seem very unattractive, but only if you do not understand the tactical use of the punch. If you are very close to your opponent, it can sometimes be your only option. And then it is both difficult to anticipate and difficult to block, a winning combination. Be wary of it: I have seen many talented martial artists surprised by a good hooking punch!

1. Start in the horse-riding stance.

2. Turn your waist to the right, allow your left arm to extend, and pull back your right elbow.

3. Twist your waist back to the left as you pull back your left elbow and punch with your right fist. Exhale on the punch.

back fist: uraken uchi

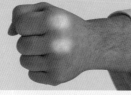

1	**Contact area**	the back of the two front knuckles
2	**Range**	short to medium
3	**Target area**	the temples; if the angle is changed, the bridge of the nose
4	**Power**	medium
5	**Speed**	fast
6	**Difficulty level**	easy
7	**Suitability for sparring**	not good because it presents a danger to the temples or the bridge of the nose; a version is sometimes used in which the karateka jumps at the opponent with a high-section back fist; check the tournament rules before using such a technique

The back-fist punch does not pack the same amount of power as the reverse punch or front punch. However, it still has enough power for specialists to use it as a destructive technique.

It is used for short- to middle-range attacks and can be used to unfold an attack from inside an opponent's guard. It is common in kata and one-step sparring, but less so in free sparring and tournament karate. The reason for this is that it can be a very dangerous technique, and is even banned from some tournaments.

The steps at the right show how to attack an opponent's temple from the ready stance.

Back-fist application: a punch to the temple.

1. Start in the ready stance, with the back of your left fist facing the right ear and your right arm extended.

2. Pull back your right elbow as you strike at temple height with the back of your fist.

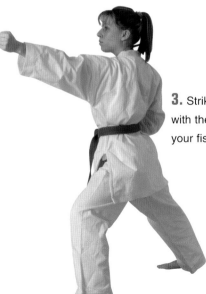

3. Strike outward with the back of your fist.

4. Withdraw your arm and assume the ready position again.

Here is how to attack the nose from the ready
stance (see heian yondan, page 206).

1. Start in the ready stance.

2. Extend your left arm and
raise your right arm.

3. Pull back your left arm as
you arc down with your right.

4. Finish the block by
snapping into position.

hammer-fist strike: tettsui uchi

1	Contact area	bottom of the fist
2	Range	short to medium
3	Target area	any part of the body
4	Power	high
5	Speed	medium-fast
6	Difficulty level	easy
7	Suitability for sparring	can be used with control, but check the rule book

The hammer-fist strike could be used to deliver a jarring blow to the head or to attack the collarbone. Other strike areas work, too, but these are the ones to watch out for in kata and one-step sparring.

This is a circular technique, which means that the momentum is not built up in a straight line, as many other techniques do, but by making a circle with your fist. It can be very powerful. A karateka with relatively little experience can use the technique destructively.

Because it is a circular technique, it can be used to great effect when attacking from inside an opponent's guard.

If the angle of attack is changed, it can be used to attack the sides of the body. Just imagine that you are using your fist like a hammer!

Hammer-fist application.

1. Start in the front stance, in the low block position.

2. Pull back as you rotate your forearm in front of your body.

3. Now step across into the horse-riding stance.

4. Strike outward with the bottom of your fist.

dynamic tensioning

Dynamic tensioning is a fairly common training technique that is applied to karate. It is an excellent method of building up power and increasing your ability to perform the kimae.

Dynamic tensioning is easy to understand. Choose a simple technique, such as the straight punch. Practice the timing of the movement a couple of times by executing fairly light punches at a slow speed. This will help you to concentrate on your timing. Make sure that you are incorporating the correct waist movements in your punching technique.

Now, rather than being soft and loose, make all of your muscles as tight as you can. Do not just tighten your fists: grip the floor with your feet, tighten your abdominal muscles, and carry the tightness through your forearms to your fists. To an observer, it will look as though you are performing a normal punch, but every muscle in your body is tight.

Keep your muscles tight and perform the punch slowly. Feel the power as one fist gradually pulls back and the other gradually pushes forward. After a few of these slow, tensioned punches, you will certainly know that you are working your muscles!

When you have done some tensioned punches, try a few normal ones. You will usually find that after working your muscles in this way, your punching gains power and coordination.

With imagination, dynamic tensioning can be applied to any hand technique.

striking

As well as punching techniques, karate has a wide variety of striking (uchi) techniques. Most of these can double up as blocking techniques. We will examine some of them here.

The aim in striking is to use one of your contact areas to attack an opponent's strike area. Many of the striking techniques come more from the realm of unarmed combat than competition. A high-powered knife-hand strike to the neck, for example, can easily result in permanent injury.

These techniques are, however, a valuable part of karate, and are vital ingredients of the karate spirit. In classes, they are studied in either kata or one-step sparring.

outside knife-hand strike:
soto shuto uchi

1	**Contact area**	the edge of the hand, on the side of the little finger
2	**Range**	medium to long
3	**Target area**	sides of the body, usually the neck or temple
4	**Power**	high
5	**Speed**	medium-fast
6	**Difficulty level**	easy
7	**Suitability for sparring**	not suitable for free sparring

Some techniques in karate are just too dangerous for free sparring. The knife-hand techniques usually fall into this category. In sparring, as in anything else, it is possible to make mistakes, and a bad mistake with a knife-hand technique can result in serious injury.

The technique uses the edge of the hand and lends itself to attacking the sides of the body. The momentum comes from a circular motion that starts either just behind your head or near your ear.

The technique can be performed as a stepping or a standing technique in any of the stances.

Outside-knife-hand-strike application.

outside knife-hand strike
from the ready stance

1. Start by assuming the lower block position.

2. Extend your left hand and raise your right hand.

3. Snap the technique into the finishing position as your left fist twists. Your right palm will be facing upward.

inside knife-hand strike: shuto uchi

1	Contact area	the edge of the hand
2	Range	medium to long
3	Target area	the side of the head or neck
4	Power	powerful
5	Speed	fast
6	Difficulty level	easy
7	Suitability for sparring	usually banned in competition

The outside knife-hand strike previously described is called an "outside" technique because it starts on the outside of the body (logical, really!). There is nothing stopping you from using the same strike from the inside of your body, when, you guessed it, it is called the inside knife-hand strike.

The technique uses the same part of the hand for striking, but the hand is the other way up at the finish. The applications are otherwise the same.

Inside-knife-hand-strike application.

inside knife-hand strike from the ready stance

1. Start by assuming the lower block position.

2. Extend your left hand and raise your right fist to head level.

3. Extend your right hand and snap into the technique as your left fist twists.

ridge hand: haito uchi

1	**Contact area**	the edge of the hand, by the thumb
2	**Range**	medium to long
3	**Target area**	the sides of the body, usually the neck or temple
4	**Power**	high
5	**Speed**	medium-fast
6	**Difficulty level**	easy
7	**Suitability for sparring**	unsuitable for free sparring

The ridge-hand technique uses the opposite side of the hand than the knife-hand technique. When you use this technique, ensure that you keep your thumb well out of the way. If you do not, you may cause yourself a painful injury, even if you are only hitting a bag.

If you are facing your opponent, the attack areas will be the neck and temples. If you are to the side of your opponent, the bridge of the nose is a good target area.

This is a very powerful technique that is frequently used for breaking wood.

Ridge-hand application.

ridge-hand strike from the ready stance

1. Start by assuming the lower block position.

2. Extend your left hand.

3. Pull back your left arm as your right arm snaps into position.

inside ridge hand

The technique shown above is for the outside ridge hand. As shown previously for the inside knife-hand strike, it is similarly possible to use it as an inside technique. Just follow the same steps that you did for the inside knife-hand strike (see pages 107 to 108).

elbowing techniques: empi uchi

Most of the punching and striking techniques shown so far have been for medium- or long-range attacks. But if your opponent comes inside that circle of attack, many of the attacks will be difficult for you to execute.

This does not mean that you are beaten, however. Your karate spirit should be stronger than that! In the inner circle, you will use your elbows and knees.

Elbow and knee attacks can be very powerful. In karate, they are not normally used for free sparring. It is true that some Thai boxers use their elbows and knees, but these fighters have usually undergone intense physical and mental conditioning to withstand the blow. Even then, it is not uncommon for injuries to occur in that environment.

There are several possible attacks to be made with the elbow. We will look at some of the more common ones here. They are usually semicircular or stabbing techniques. The main difference between them is the direction in which they travel. They are all devastating!

1	Contact area	the edge or point of the elbow
2	Range	close to medium
3	Power	very high
4	Speed	medium-fast
5	Difficulty level	easy
6	Suitability for sparring	unsuitable for free sparring

upper elbow strike: jodan empi uchi

The upper, or upward, elbow strike follows very similar dynamics to a punch. If it helps in the beginning, imagine this technique as punching with your elbow.

It uses the edge of the elbow to connect with the point of the opponent's chin.

Upper elbow-strike application.

1. First assume the attention position.

2. Extend your left fist. Then pull it back as your right fist starts to travel forward.

Power your right elbow into a high finishing position as your left fist snaps to your waist.

middle elbow strike:
chudan empi uchi

The middle elbow strike is made to an opponent's floating rib or solar plexus, depending on how he or she is facing you.

Middle elbow-strike application.

1. Extend your left hand in the lower block position.

2. Step across into the horse-riding stance and cross your arms.

3. Separate your arms with a snap. Your right fist should finish moving at your belt.

reverse middle elbow strike: ushiro chudan empi uchi

This strike uses the point of the elbow to attack an opponent who is behind you. It will hit the attacker in either the solar plexus or the ribs.

The hand of the arm whose elbow is being used for the attack is clenched into a fist. The palm of the other hand is placed on top of the fist to give it extra strength and drive the attack home.

Reverse middle elbow-strike application.

1. Extend your left fist in the lower block position.

2. Place your right hand over your left fist. Twist your body.

3. Drive the attack home with a waist movement.

other strikes

The strikes described here are by no means all of the vast range of strikes available to the advanced karateka. They do, however, demonstrate the mechanics of how most strikes are performed.

Once you have grasped the mechanics of the movement, it is possible to learn new strikes just by knowing the part of the body that you are striking with, what you are striking at, and having an idea of how it is done.

Here is a brief introduction to some of the other strikes that are used in karate.

1. Spear finger thrust: nukite.

2. Knuckle fist: hiraken.

3. Palm-heel strike: teisho uchi.

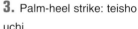

Striking area for spear finger thrust.

Striking area for knuckle fist.

Striking area for palm-heel strike.

1	Uses the tips of the fingers together
2	Usually aimed at the neck or solar plexus
3	Uses the same kind of action as a punch

1	Strikes with the knuckles
2	Aims at the neck
3	Similar action to the punch

1	Uses the heel of the hand
2	Can aim at the jaw or solar plexus
3	Similar action to the punch

blocking

It is possible to argue that blocking (uke) is a more important skill than attacking in martial arts. If you were able to evade or block every one of your opponent's attacks, then you would have successfully defended yourself. I do not think that any martial-art style uses this as its tactical philosophy, but it is a useful concept for underlining the importance of blocking.

The ultimate way of blocking an attack is simply not to be where the attack is. This can be done by side-steps and evasions. However, it may be that you need to get close to your opponent to counterattack, as when sparring, or that your opponent's attack cannot be neutralized by evasion and side-stepping.

In this situation, you will need to find a way of deflecting the attack. This is usually done with the forearm, although it is possible to use other parts of the body, such as the knee or elbow, to block an attack.

When learning blocking, think about what you will do after you have performed the block. This should always be to try to set up your opponent for your counterattack.

Blocks can be made to the high area (jodan), middle area (chudan), or low area (gedan). Taking these three body areas and other considerations into account, there is a wide range of blocks available to the karateka. We shall now examine some of them.

The downward block, or gedan barai, is a fundamental blocking technique.

downward block: gedan barai

The downward block is probably the most basic karate technique. It is absolutely intrinsic to the way that karate works. For this reason, it is usually taught to karateka very early in their training, and yet is still included in more advanced kata.

This block uses the bottom of the fist or the outer forearm to strike the opponent's attack and knock it out of the way. You will usually see this block being performed in the front stance. It can also be done in any of the other stances.

A typical application for this block would be to defend against a lower front kick, as shown on the right. Do not get stuck on this idea, though. What is to stop you from using exactly the same technique as a lower hammer-fist strike to the opponent's inside leg or groin?

When blocking, do not try to hit your opponent's fist or foot as it is all too easy to miss that target. It is better to use the block against your opponent's forearm or lower leg.

The downward block in action.

This block can also be used as a strike.

downward block:
gedan barai

1. Start in the ready stance.

2. Point your right fist downward and raise your left fist to your ear as you start to step forward.

3. Drive your left arm down and pull your right arm back as you step. Finish with a twist of your hips in the front stance, extending your left arm into the lower block.

upward block: age uke

The second of the basic karate blocks is the upper block, or age uke. While the downward block protects the lower-groin area, this block protects the upper-head area.

It can be used to protect yourself against a kick or punch coming toward your face, as shown on the top right.

A more advanced way of performing this block is to use it as an entangled-arm lock. In this sequence, the attacker comes toward you and you use the arm that would normally be the reaction arm to deflect the attack. You then follow straight through to take your opponent's elbow. When you have the elbow, you can step through and use the block as a throw if you want.

The upward block in action.

This block can also be used as a strike.

upper block

1. Start in the lower block position.

2. Step forward with your right leg and raise your right arm.

3. Cross your arms in front of your chest, with your right hand clenched into a fist.

4. Snap your right arm into position as you pull your left hand back to your belt.

inner-forearm block: uchi ude uke

So far, we have looked at defending the upper-head area and the lower-groin area. Obviously, there is a part in the middle that we need to protect, too!

The two most basic blocks for the middle section are the inner-forearm block and the outer-forearm block. For the inner-forearm block, we use the forearm on the thumb side to deflect an attack.

Torsion of the waist and correct timing for the reaction hand generate the power for the inner- and outer-forearm blocks. Rotating the forearm at the end of the block adds power in the same way that rotating your fist at the end of a punch gives power.

The inner-forearm block is useful because it tends to open up the attacker ready for your counterattack.

The inner-forearm block in action.

This block can also be used as a strike.

inner-forearm block

1. Start in the lower block position.

2. Step up with your right leg as you extend your left arm.

3. Step forward with your right leg into the front stance.

4. Snap your arms into the blocking position.

outer-forearm block: soto ude uke

The outer-forearm block works in a similar way to the inner-forearm block. Instead of opening up the opponent, however, it forces the opponent's attack to cross his or her own body. This makes it difficult for your opponent to follow with another attack, and you still have plenty of target areas that you can hit.

In this block, we use the little-finger side of the forearm to knock the opponent's attack out of the way. Another application of this block could be to use it like a hammer-fist strike to the temple. The mechanics are the same, but you just aim a little higher and change the focus of your mind from blocking to striking.

The outer-forearm block in action.

This block can also be used as an attack.

outer-forearm block

1. Start in the lower block position.

2. Raise your right arm and extend your left arm. Step up with your right leg.

3. Step forward into the front stance and snap into the blocking position.

augmented-forearm block: morote uke

So far, we have looked at the four basic blocks in karate. There are many more blocks available to the karateka than just four, however. Others include the knife-hand-guarding block, the X-block, the vertical knife-hand-guarding block, and the augmented-forearm block.

All of these blocks, and some others, are demonstrated in the section on karate katas (starting on page 149). If you understand the basic concepts behind, and mechanics of, the four basic blocks, along with the fundamentals of punching, you should have little difficulty figuring out how the other blocks work and their individual tactical advantages.

A block that is slightly outside the frame of the other blocks is the augmented-forearm block. It is unusual because you use both arms to block on one side. If you imagine that you are up against a powerful kicker, then a simple one-armed block may sometimes not be strong enough to stop a full-on, roundhouse kick. Obviously, it would be better not to have let the kick happen, or to be out of its way, but life is not always like that!

In this situation, the augmented-forearm block is a good block to use. It is similar to the inner-forearm block, but the fist of the non-blocking arm touches your forearm just inside the elbow. This makes the block much more rigid because it is supported by your other arm.

Although the block is very strong, you still have to be careful with your timing and aim. If you let the kicker aim a full-force roundhouse kick at your forearm when it is supported in such a way, it will probably stop the kick, but may also damage your arm. Use your understanding of the kick to try to hit the attacking leg in a safer place.

The augmented-forearm block in action.

This block can also be used as a strike to move your opponent away.

augmented-forearm block

1. Start in the front stance, with your left leg forward and your left arm in the lower blocking position.

2. Step forward with your right foot, placing it close to your left foot as you lower your arms.

3. Step forward as you push outward with your left fist.

4. Sink into the front stance as you snap your left arm across and your right fist flicks up so that it touches your inner forearm.

kicking

If you look at the covers of most martial-arts books and magazines, you will see a picture of somebody executing a kick (geri). If you watch a martial-arts film, then the chances are that the hero will be a "kicker." (Indeed, some well-known martial-arts actors are renowned for their ability to perform high kicks on set.)

The simple reason for this is that kicks look good. A well-executed kick has an aesthetic quality that hints at the martial artist's power, balance, and training.

But kicks don't just look good. In practical styles like karate, nothing is included for aesthetic reasons only. A good kick can be a fast and powerful attack that can cover a long range. A simple front kick hits the target.

Now think about the power behind the kick. Look at the muscles in your arms compared to those in your legs. Most people have at least twice the muscle development in their legs as in their arms. It comes in handy for walking!

But a kick is not just about the legs. You should use the whole of your body to drive power through a kick. You need to understand which part of the foot you are kicking with and the target area that you can hit with it.

The kicks that follow are some of the basic ones. Nearly all kicks can be performed as jumping kicks for added range and height. Some styles kick with the leading leg for extra speed, and others do not.

Kicks are an important aspect of karate. They help you to develop poise and suppleness.

Kicking for a few minutes is also good cardiovascular training. Any karateka can vouch for that! However, do not be lured into thinking that karate is all about kicking. This is just one aspect of a varied art form.

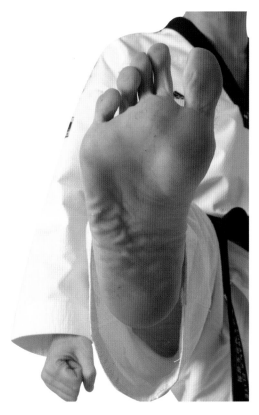

Karate teaches you which part of the foot it's best to kick with.

front kick: mae geri

1	**Contact area**	the ball of the foot
2	**Range**	long
3	**Power**	high
4	**Speed**	fast
5	**Difficulty level**	easy
6	**Suitability for sparring**	highly suitable for free sparring

If you imagine a soccer player taking a penalty, he will use a version of the front kick. The difference is that he will be kicking at the center of a ball, 6 inches (15 centimeters) above the ground, and the karateka will be aiming at a much higher target.

The kick is fast, powerful, and versatile. It can be aimed at either the middle section or the high section in sparring, and at the legs in self-defense.

Front-kick application.

The power of the kick comes from the hips, and not just from the flick of the knee. The knee is lifted quickly and the ball of the foot is shot outward in a whiplash-type of motion. As you kick out with your foot, you simultaneously drive your hips forward for power. After the kick, it is important to bring your foot back as fast as you fired it out so that your leg cannot easily be caught and your knee is protected from damage.

When making the kick, you must use your hips to power your leg. If you can do this, then your kicks will develop great power.

It is possible to perform the front kick as a jumping kick. That kick is analyzed on pages 146 to 147.

1. Start in the fighting stance.

2. Step forward.

3. Lift your knee.

4. Kick out with the ball of your foot.

5. Withdraw your leg.

6. Now put your foot down in the fighting-stance position.

roundhouse kick: mawashi geri

1	Contact area	the ball of the foot or instep
2	Range	long
3	Power	high
4	Speed	fast
5	Difficulty level	medium
6	Suitability for sparring	highly suitable for free sparring

The roundhouse kick is very popular in sparring and kata work. The reason for this is its high power and speed.

The path of the roundhouse kick is circular, and it attacks from the side. It is therefore common to try to use the kick as a high kick to the side of the head. In competition, it is also possible to score a point by kicking to the midsection, that is, if the technique is clean and hits the target properly.

Roundhouse-kick application using the instep.

In the traditional roundhouse kick, you will make contact with the ball of the foot. This makes the kick very powerful, and this method is sometimes used for breaking boards in demonstrations or gradings.

In sparring and competitions, it is more common to use the instep of the foot. This allows the karateka to use exactly the same technique, but in a slightly less destructive way. If somebody hits you with the instep of the foot it will hurt, but not as much as if he or she had used the ball of the foot.

To perform the roundhouse kick, you lift the knee of the kicking leg and pivot around on the other foot. The higher you lift your knee, the higher your kick will be. When you release the kick, power is transmitted from your hips. After the release, you should quickly bring your foot back.

There is a reverse version of the roundhouse kick that is discussed on pages 143 to 145. It is also possible to execute the roundhouse kick as a jumping, or a jumping and spinning, kick.

Start in the front stance, with your left leg forward.

1. Shift your weight forward onto your left leg and lift the knee of your right leg.

2. Pivot around on your left foot and release your right foot to execute the kick.

3. Lift your knee.

4. Extend your leg into the kicking position.

5. Withdraw your kicking foot.

6. Finish in the fighting stance.

side-thrust kick:
yoko geri kekomi

1	Contact area	the side of the foot
2	Range	long
3	Power	very high
4	Speed	fast
5	Difficulty level	medium
6	Suitability for sparring	highly suitable for free sparring

The side-thrust kick is a very powerful kick. In a way, it is like punching with the edge of your foot. The strength of your leg and the motion that is carried through from your body give the kick a powerfully piercing quality.

In traditional kata, the target for the side-thrust kick is frequently the neck. The neck is a target that would be avoided in sparring, however.

In sparring, side-thrust kicks can be used as straight kicks to the midsection or head.

Side-thrust-kick application.

The side-thrust kick is a useful technique for stopping an aggressive attacker. In sparring, some fighters consider attack the best form of defense. These fighters sometimes try to rush at their opponents, making it difficult for them to attack. One good way of stopping this sort of attack is with a well-placed side-thrust kick. Make sure that your balance is good, though, otherwise you may be knocked over!

The side-thrust kick can be performed in any stance. To execute it, the knee is raised and the kick is delivered by twisting the waist. As always, you should bring your foot back as quickly as possible after making the kick.

The side kick could also be used as a thrusting kick, depending upon the way that you use your kicking leg. For the thrusting kick, your body will usually lean into the kick more.

1. Start in the back stance.

2. Open your front foot.

3. Lift your knee in front of your body.

4. Pivot around on your standing leg.

5. Thrust your foot out with a twist of your hips.

6. Quickly bring your foot back again.

7. Put your foot on the floor.

8. Finish in the fighting stance.

crescent kick:
mikazuki geri

1	**Contact area**	the flat of the foot
2	**Range**	long
3	**Power**	medium
4	**Speed**	fast
5	**Difficulty level**	easy
6	**Suitability for sparring**	highly suitable for free sparring

In the crescent kick, your foot swings around in an arc. The idea is to try to hit your opponent on the side of the head with your foot. Some styles use the flat of the foot for the impact area, while others use the ball of the foot. It all depends on the application being used.

If you are using the crescent kick as a block, then you will use the flat of your foot. If you are in a sparring situation, you will also use the flat of your foot. In some kata, the ball of the foot is used to create more destructive power.

Crescent-kick application.

The crescent kick is quite popular in sparring as it can sometimes come from the side and take an opponent off guard.

There are many variations of the crescent kick. In the variation shown here, the foot travels inward from outside the body. It is also possible to perform the crescent kick the other way around, traveling outward. With both of these variations, you could also execute a jumping, or a jumping and spinning, kick. These are highly aggressive kicks. If you use them in semi-contact sparring, you will need to be careful that you do not use excessive force.

The power for the crescent kick comes mainly from the thigh muscles. You use these muscles, backed by waist movement, to swing your leg in an arc and make the kick.

1. Start in the back stance.

2. Shift your weight onto your front leg and lift your back heel.

3. Pivot around on the ball of your standing foot as you make the kick.

4. Flick your kicking leg outward in an arc.

5. Return to the "chambered" position.

6. Finish in the fighting stance.

back kick: ushiro geri

1	**Contact area**	the heel
2	**Range**	long
3	**Power**	very powerful
4	**Speed**	fast
5	**Difficulty level**	medium
6	**Suitability for sparring**	highly suitable for free sparring

When you perform the back kick, it is easy to put the whole of your body weight behind the kick, making it very powerful. If you are using it in a semi-contact tournament, you will need to take care that you do not use excessive force.

The back kick feels similar to the side-thrust kick, so be sure that you know the difference if it is in your grading! The big differ-

Back-kick application.

ence is that you will turn through 180 degrees to execute a back kick, and you will hit with your heel.

The back kick is a good kick to follow a side-thrust kick. The way that the side-thrust kick turns your body means that you have to turn only a little farther to perform the back kick.

The back kick can also be performed as a jumping, spinning kick. This is quite a difficult kick, and it is hard for an inexperienced karateka to regulate the power. Unless you are confident with the jumping kick, it is best to exercise caution in semi-contact tournaments.

The back kick is a useful kick to master. It is very powerful and comes at an awkward angle to block. It is therefore excellent for striking an opponent's middle area, especially if it is improperly guarded.

1. Start in the back stance, with your right leg behind.

2. Step across with your right leg.

3. Pivot on your feet through a 180-degree turn.

4. Raise your right knee.

5. Thrust backwards with your right heel.

6. Return your knee to the raised position.

7. Pivot around on your standing leg.

8. Finish in the fighting stance.

reverse roundhouse kick: ushiro mawashi geri

1	**Contact area**	the heel
2	**Range**	long
3	**Power**	medium
4	**Speed**	fast
5	**Difficulty level**	difficult
6	**Suitability for sparring**	highly suitable for free sparring

The reverse, or back, roundhouse kick is the most difficult kick described in this book. The mechanics of the kick are straightforward: you spin your body around and use the momentum to throw back the heel of your foot for the kick.

What makes the kick difficult is that you have to turn away from your opponent to build up the power. This can make aiming more difficult, especially if your opponent is moving. However, with practice, this kick can be done very

Reverse-roundhouse-kick application.

quickly, and performers of the kick find it highly efficient for scoring points in tournaments.

In tournaments, the flat of the foot is usually used to prevent serious injury to an opponent, for the kick is usually aimed at his or her head.

It is possible to perform this kick as a jumping kick, but as you can imagine, you will need to be very proficient at the normal version before trying a more advanced jumping kick.

As with all kicks, if you want to get it right, you'll need to practice it!

1. Start in the back stance.

2. Step across with your right leg.

3. Twist your body and look over your shoulder.

4. Raise the knee of your kicking leg.

5. Flick back your heel for the kick.

6. Control your leg after making the kick.

7. Finish in the fighting stance.

jumping front kick:
tobi mae geri

1	Contact area	the ball of the foot
2	Range	very long
3	Power	high
4	Speed	fast
5	Difficulty level	medium to difficult
6	Suitability for sparring	highly suitable for free sparring

The jumping front kick is quite a spectacular kick that is surprisingly easy to perform. As long as you can perform the basic front kick fairly well, then you stand a good chance of succeeding with the jumping front kick. Indeed, being able to execute the jumping front kick may even improve your standing front kick.

Why jump with a kick? Apart from improving your coordination and kicking repertoire, there are some good tactical reasons.

First, if you need to make your kick higher, jump! Second, some fighters stand well back from an attacker and try to pick their moment to attack. If you are up against one of these, a jumping kick will sometimes give you the range that you need to get at him or her.

The only difference between kicking for height and kicking for distance is the way that you jump: high or far.

It is possible to perform the jumping front kick with either the loading leg or the back leg. The basic procedure is the same.

Jumping-front-kick application.

1. Start in the fighting stance.

2. Lift your non-kicking leg as high as you can.

3. Chamber your kicking leg.

4. Extend into the kick.

5. Land on your non-kicking leg.

6. Settle into the fighting stance.

chapter 6 **kata**

So far we have looked at a selection of the techniques that are used in karate. There are many more techniques, however, as well as different ways of performing a technique.

Who would have thought that there were so many variations of the punch? Indeed, skilled karateka can view most parts of their bodies as weapons. A little finger delivered to the correct place at the correct time, for example, can cause a devastating blow!

So how do we learn all of these techniques? One of the old ways was to learn just one technique and to practice it, sometimes for years, until the sensei or master was satisfied that the pupil was ready to learn the next piece of karate knowledge.

Can you imagine trying to do that? Practicing the same punch for about five years? These days, it simply would not happen. Techniques and methods have moved on. But think about the concept. There is a feeling within some karate schools, especially the more Zen-orientated ones, that this is not such a bad idea. If you have complete mastery of one technique, it will be devastating. And from that one technique, all of the other techniques will also flow.

As you can no doubt imagine, different masters had different ideas through the ages. Nowadays, most traditional martial arts use kata. "Kata" means pattern or form. Kata are used by nearly all of the other martial-art styles, no matter where they are from. Ju jitsu, judo, tai chi, wing chun, and tae kwon do all regard kata as a basic building block, for instance.

Most of the kata have the "one-technique" idea embedded in them. The old masters were very crafty when designing the kata. For example, our first kata, taikyoku shodan, is the key to mastering shotokan karate. If you can perform all of the techniques in this kata to a very high skill level, you will be an excellent karateka.

improving your kata

Engravings and murals show that kata were being practiced around a thousand years ago. Many of the kata that exist today evolved from these old patterns and forms. And many of the techniques shown are familiar to the modern martial artist.

Apart from learning something that stretches back into history, you are learning something that people have valued for an immensely long time in human terms. How much of today's culture will be similar in the year 3000?

For something to last that long, there must be some real substance to it, which surely makes it worth the effort of getting it right.

So what do we look for in our kata? In a very real way, the learning of kata is a spiritual experience. This is the dimension that transforms your kata into something worthwhile. In martial arts, the path to the spirit is the body. The different elements of the kata would have a lesser effect on their own. The joining of the elements leads to the transformation.

There are some things to focus on.

body alignment

Is your body aligned in the most efficient way? For example, if your front stance is leaning to one side, you cannot deliver maximum power. The laws of physics will be against you because gravity will always try to pull you into the worst direction for a karateka. If your body is in alignment, the energy meridians are open and ki can flow.

balance

The question of balance is related to body alignment. If your body is aligned, then it is balanced. But it is not just about your body. If your mind and body are not balanced, then you are not balanced physically. For example, if you are thinking about the next technique before finishing the one that you are performing, you will tend to lean into the technique, thus upsetting your alignment and balance.

If your technique is correct, and you are striking or blocking the correct parts, you are starting to control your body with your mind.

Smooth breathing and delivery of power are indications that you have started to balance such internal and external factors.

no mind

Balance leads directly to the concept of "no mind," or "the empty space." In kata, you should think about the movement that you are performing. Not the one that you just did or the coming one. This means that you need to be balanced between the past and the future. This

is what the meditation experts call the "here and now." Learning to experience the moment as it is leads to a profound state of meditation, and kata can help you to get there.

Do not mistake this for some kind of trance. The karateka must show very great spirit and an extreme level of alertness. The power of the kiai and the focus of the eyes are clear indicators that the spirit is strong.

first kata: taikyoku shodan

In the philosophy of karate, taikyoku represents the idea of the universe in its primal state. According to this concept, the universe started as a unity and split between heaven and Earth. Taikyoku represents that original state.

Taikyoku shodan therefore represents the karateka in the beginning stages. It is the most elementary of the katas, and therefore the most important. It is common for the karateka who reaches the black-belt level to revisit this kata. This gives more advanced students the chance to review their basic techniques in the light of a more complete understanding of the art.

The kata requires that you learn one block, one stance, and one attack.

The full kata, including transitional moves, is explained first. A quick reference summary is provided on pages 160 to 161.

1. Start in yoi, the ready stance.

2. Simultaneously look to the left, slide back your left foot, raise your left fist, and project your right fist forward.

3. Twist your body into the zenkutsu dachi, or the front stance, while executing the hidari gedan barai, or left lower block.

4. Project your left fist forward as you bring your right foot close to your left foot. Keep your right fist clenched close to your belt.

5. Step forward into the front stance while simultaneously punching with your right hand and pulling back your left fist for the migi oi zuki, or right stepping punch.

6. Slide back your right foot as you look back over your right shoulder and raise your right fist. Project your left fist forward.

7. Turn through 180 degrees by twisting into a front stance. At the same time, block downward with your right hand for the migi gedan barai, or right lower block.

8. Project your right fist forward as you bring your left foot close to your right foot. Keep your fists clenched.

9. Step forward with your left foot into the front stance. Punch with your left hand for the hidari oi zuki, or left stepping punch.

10. Step across with your left leg and turn to face forward. Prepare for a lower block by raising your left fist and extending your right fist.

11. Twist your body into the front stance and execute the hidari gedan barai, or left lower block.

12. Step up with your right leg in preparation for punching.

13. Step forward in the front stance for the migi oi zuki, or right stepping punch.

14. Step up with your left leg in preparation for punching with your left fist.

15. Step forward in the front stance for the hidari oi zuki, or left stepping punch.

16. Step up with your right leg to prepare for punching.

17. Move into the front stance for the migi oi zuki, or right stepping punch. Shout a loud "kiai!"

18. Step across with your left leg in preparation for making a lower block to your left side with your left hand.

19. Execute the hidari gedan barai, or left lower block, from the front stance.

20. Step up with your right leg in preparation for punching with your right fist.

21. Execute the migi oi zuki, or right stepping punch, in the front stance.

22. Slide back your right leg in preparation for a 180-degree turn and block.

23. Move into the front stance for the migi gedan barai, or right lower block.

24. Step up with your left leg.

25. Step forward with your left leg into the front stance and punch with your left hand for the hidari oi zuki.

26. Slide your left leg across in preparation for a lower block (made facing away from the camera here).

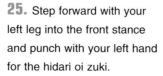

27. Twist into the front stance for a hidari gedan barai, or left lower block.

28. Step up with your right leg in preparation for punching.

29. Move your right leg forward into the front stance for a migi oi zuki, or right stepping punch.

30. Step up with your left leg, ready to punch.

31. Step into a hidari oi zuki, or left stepping punch, in the front stance.

32. Step up with your right leg.

33. Perform a migi oi zuki, or right stepping punch, in the front stance with a loud "kiai!"

34. Slide back your left foot in preparation for another lower block. Note that for this turn, your body will move through 270 degrees (a three-quarter turn).

35. Execute a hidari gedan barai, or left lower block, in the front stance.

36. Step forward to prepare to punch with the left fist.

37. Execute a migi oi zuki, or right stepping punch, with your right fist.

38. Slide back your right foot, turn your body through 180 degrees, and prepare to make a lower block.

39. Execute a migi gedan barai, or right lower block, in the front stance.

40. Step up with your left leg to prepare for a final punch.

41. Execute a hidari oi zuki, or left stepping punch.

42. Slide back your left foot into a position where it is level with your right foot.

43. Finish the kata in the yame, or finishing position.

taikyoku shodan: summary

The main movements of the taikyoku shodan kata are shown here without the transitional movements as a quick reference guide.

1. Ready stance.

2. Quarter-turn, low block.

3. Punch.

4. Half-turn, low block.

5. Punch.

6. Quarter-turn, low block.

7. Punch.

8. Punch.

9. Punch with "kiai!"

10. Quarter-turn, low block.

11. Punch.

12. Half-turn, low block.

13. Punch.

14. Quarter-turn, low block.

15. Punch.

16. Punch.

17. Punch with "kiai!"

18. Three-quarter-turn, low block.

19. Punch.

20. Half-turn, low block.

21. Punch.

22. Finishing position.

applications for taikyoku shodan

The applications for taikyoku shodan are relatively straightforward and easy to understand on a basic level. When practicing the kata, you should always visualize the application and think about where you are striking and the part of the body that you are striking with.

The applications shown here are those taught to the beginner. On a more advanced level, it is possible to use the blocks as strikes and vice versa. It is also possible to view some of the turns as throws.

application number 1

Below we see the lower block being used to stop a front kick. Note how the outer edge of the forearm is being used to stop the kick. Also note that the block is being aimed at the leg, *not* the foot.

This is a basic application. Try to think of others to expand your awareness of the technique. Practice them and see if they work. Discuss your findings with your instructor.

Movement number 3 from the taikyoku shodan kata.

application number 2

Obviously, karate is not all about blocking. After a block comes the retaliatory strike.

Below we see the most basic strike, the punch, being used. Note how the two front knuckles find their target.

Movement number 5 from the taikyoku shodan kata.

second kata: heian shodan

The word "heian" translates as "peaceful mind." It is part of the philosophy of all traditional martial arts that the mind must be focused and quiet to attain skill. In a real combat situation, can you imagine somebody trying to defend himself or herself while thinking about what he or she will be having for dinner?

In kata practice, you should have the same focus. Your mind should be quiet, peaceful, and focused. An experienced instructor, or sensei, will be able to tell from your performance if you have learned how to focus your mind on your kata in this way.

Just as in meditation, there are various levels when it comes to attaining this peace of mind. There are five heian kata that increase in complexity. After you have learned to achieve inner peace while practicing one of them, your learning will increase when you move on to the next, more complex, kata.

The heian shodan introduces the knife-hand block, rising block, and hammer-fist strike.

The full kata, including transitional moves, is explained first. A quick reference summary is provided on pages 172 to 173.

1. Start in yoi, the ready stance.

2. Simultaneously look to the left, slide back your left foot, raise your left fist, and project your right fist forward.

3. Twist your body into the zenkutsu dachi, or front stance, while executing the hidari gedan barai, or left lower block.

4. Project your left fist forward as you bring your right foot close to your left foot. Keep your right fist clenched close to your belt.

5. Step forward into the front stance while simultaneously punching with your right hand and pulling back your left fist for the migi oi zuki, or right stepping punch.

6. Slide back your right foot as you look back over your right shoulder and raise your right fist. Project your left fist forward.

7. Turn 180 degrees by twisting into the front stance. Simultaneously block downward with your right hand for the migi gedan barai, or right lower block.

8. With your weight on your left leg, draw back your right foot. Pull back your right hand in a large arc, twisting your forearm as you pull it back.

9. Continue the arc for the migi tettsui uchi, or hammer-fist strike.

10. Prepare to punch with your left hand.

11. Execute a hidari oi zuki, or left stepping punch, punching while stepping into the front stance.

12. Pull your left leg across the front of your body and prepare for a lower block.

13. Execute a hidari gedan barai, or left lower block, with your left hand.

14. Prepare for an upper block by drawing your right foot close to your left foot and opening your left hand.

15. Execute a migi age uke, or right upper block, with your right arm.

16. Draw your left leg close to your right and prepare for an upper block with your left arm.

17. Execute a hidari age uke, or left upper block, with your left arm.

18. Again prepare to make an upper block with your right arm.

19. Execute a migi age uke, or right upper block, with a loud "kiai!"

20. Sweep your left, rear leg forward so that your body makes a three-quarter-turn in preparation for a lower block.

21. Execute a hidari gedan barai, or left lower block.

22. Step up to prepare for a punch.

23. Perform a migi oi zuki, or right stepping punch, in the front stance.

24. Sweep back your right foot to turn your body 180 degrees and prepare for a lower block.

25. Execute a migi gedan barai, or right lower block, in the front stance.

26. Step up to prepare to make a punch with your left fist.

27. Execute a hidari oi zuki, or left stepping punch, with your left fist.

28. Sweep your left leg across to prepare for a lower block (made facing away from the camera here).

29. Execute a hidari gedan barai, or left lower block, with your left arm.

30. Prepare to punch with your right fist.

31. Perform a migi oi zuki, or right stepping punch, with your right fist.

32. Prepare to punch and then execute a hidari oi zuki, or left stepping punch.

33. Prepare to punch with your right fist.

34. Execute a migi oi zuki, or right stepping punch, with a loud "kiai!"

35. Sweep your left, rear foot to your right, so that your body turns 270 degrees, with both hands open.

36. Execute a hidari shuto uke, or left knife-hand block, in the back stance.

37. Step up with your left foot, extend your left arm, and bring your right hand close to your neck.

38. Perform a migi shuto uke, or right knife-hand block, in the back stance at an angle of 45 degrees.

39. Sweep your right foot across and prepare for another knife-hand block.

40. Execute a migi shuto uke, or right knife-hand block, in the back stance.

41. Prepare for the next knife-hand block by bringing your left foot closer to your right and extending your right arm while raising your left.

42. Perform a hidari shuto uke, or left knife-hand block, at an angle of 45 degrees.

43. Slide back your left foot into a position where it is level with your right foot.

44. Finish the kata in the yame, or finishing position.

heian shodan: summary

The main movements of the heian shodan kata are shown here without the transitional movements as a quick reference guide.

1. Ready stance.

2. Quarter-turn, low block.

3. Punch.

4. Half-turn, low block.

5. Hammer-fist strike.

6. Punch.

7. Quarter-turn, low block.

8. Upper block.

9. Upper block.

10. Upper block with "kiai!"

11. Three-quarter-turn, low block.

12. Punch.

13. Half-turn, low block.

14. Punch.

15. Quarter-turn, low block.

16. Punch.

17. Punch.

18. Punch with "kiai!"

19. Quarter-turn, knife-hand block.

20. 45-degree turn, knife-hand block.

21. 135-degree turn, knife-hand block.

22. 45-degree turn, knife-hand block.

23. Finishing position.

applications for heian shodan

The following are some of the new applications that appear in this kata. Do not forget the applications that you learned for taikyoku shodan as they also appear in this kata. (This advice applies to all of the later kata, too.)

application number 1

A common misconception with karate is that it is solely comprised of kicking and punching. This may be true for the absolute beginner, but the advanced student can use many of the techniques for locks and throws. Do not forget the roots of karate!

Below, the upper rising block is being used as a locking technique against the opponent's elbow. If sufficient power were applied, the elbow would break, so be careful!

A less obvious application of movement number 8 from the heian shodan kata.

application number 2

Below, the knife-hand block is being used to strike the neck. It could also be used to strike the wrist or ankle if you need a block.

This is a basic application. Try to think of others to expand your awareness of the technique. Practice them and see if they work. Discuss your findings with your instructor.

Movement number 36 from the heian shodan kata used as a strike.

third kata: heian nidan

In the previous kata, heian shodan, we discussed the idea of being "peaceful" within the kata. This is not about performing the kata with no intent—far from it! It is about focusing the mind so that the intent is stronger.

The example that we looked at was how the mind can wander when performing kata. With some practice, you should be able to prevent thoughts about your next meal from intruding on your kata. But what should you think of while performing your kata?

The answer is the application. If you can focus your mind on the application that you are demonstrating within the kata, then you are working along the right lines. But what about the next move? When you can practice the kata so that the next move comes without you thinking about it, then you will have reached another level of inner peace.

The heian nidan kata uses the back stance introduced in the heian shodan [move]. It also introduces the front kick, side-snapping kick, close punch, back fist, and spear-finger thrust.

The full kata, including transitional moves, is explained first. A quick reference summary is provided on pages 188 to 190.

1. Start in yoi, the ready stance.

2. Step across with your left leg into the back stance and drop your arms below your belt.

3. Snap up your arms into a position where your right forearm is guarding your face and your left forearm is working like an upper block (hidari jodan, or left upper block, with haiwan uke, or back-arm block).

4. Prepare for close punch.

5. Perform a migi ura zuki, or close punch, with your right hand.

6. Prepare to make a hammer-fist strike.

7. Perform a hammer-fist strike with your left hand.

8. Shift your weight onto your left leg to turn through 180 degrees. Drop both arms.

9. Snap your arms upward so that this time your left arm blocks your head and your right arm protects your face. (Migi jodan with haiwan uke.)

10. Prepare to make a close punch with your left fist.

11. Execute a close punch with your left fist (hidari ura zuki).

12. Prepare to make a hammer-fist strike.

13. Make a back fist with your right fist (migi tettsui uke).

14. Slide forward your left foot in preparation for making the side-snapping kick.

Front view.

15. Execute a side-snapping kick with your right leg and a simultaneous back fist with your right fist (yoko keage-uraken).

16. Turn your head as you come out of the side kick and prepare to knife-hand block.

17. Knife-hand block with your left hand (hidari shuto uke) in the back stance, with your right leg supporting your weight.

18. Step up with your right leg and prepare your arms for another knife-hand block.

19. Knife-hand block with your right hand (migi shuto uke) in the back stance, with your left leg supporting your weight.

20. Step up with your left leg and prepare your arms for another knife-hand block.

21. Knife-hand block with your left hand (hidari shuto uke) in the back stance, with your right leg supporting your weight.

22. Step through with your right leg and position your right thumb so that it is pointing down in preparation for the spear-finger thrust.

23. Spear-finger thrust to the solar plexus with the right hand (migi chudan shihon nukite) in the front stance with a loud "kiai!"

24. Slide your left foot across, turning your body through 270 degrees in preparation for a knife-hand guarding block.

25. Perform a knife-hand guarding block with your left hand (hidari shuto uke) in the back stance.

26. Draw your right foot to the left and prepare your arms to make another guarding block.

27. Make a knife-hand guarding block with your right hand, at a 45-degree angle to the previous one, in the back stance.

28. Slide back your right foot to turn your body around and prepare for another knife-hand guarding block.

29. Perform a knife-hand guarding block with your right arm in the back stance.

30. Draw your left foot to the right and prepare your arms for another guarding block.

Front view.

Front view.

31. Perform a knife-hand guarding block, at a 45-degree angle to the previous one, using your left hand in the back stance.

32. Use your left foot to step across into the front stance, with the palm of your right hand facing downward.

Front view.

Front view.

33. Perform a migi gyaki haito uke block with your right hand.

34. Follow with a reverse outer block with your right hand (migi gyaku uchi uke).

Front view.

35. Raise your right knee for a front kick.

Front view.

36. Extend the ball of your right foot into a front kick (migi mae geri).

Front view.

37. Release your foot from the kick.

Front view.

38. Step forward into a left-hand reverse punch (hidari chudan gyaki zuki).

Front view.

Front view.

39. Cross your left arm over your body in preparation for a block.

40. Block with your left forearm (hidari uchi uke), with the motion traveling outward.

Front view.

Front view.

41. Raise your left knee ready for a front kick.

42. Extend your left leg into the kick (hidari mae geri).

Front view.

43. Release the kick.

Front view.

44. Step down to execute a reverse punch with your right fist (migi gyaku zuki).

Front view.

45. Prepare to perform an augmented block.

Front view.

46. Execute an augmented block with your right arm (migi morote uke).

47. Slide your left foot across so that your body turns through 270 degrees and prepare to perform a low block.

48. Execute a low block with your left arm (hidari gedan barai).

49. Draw your right foot toward your left foot and prepare to perform an upper block.

50. Execute the upper block with your right arm (migi age uke) at a 45-degree angle to the previous block.

51. Step across with your right foot and prepare for a lower block.

52. Perform a lower block with your right arm (migi gedan barai).

53. Draw your left foot to your right in preparation for an upper block.

54. Execute an upper block with your left arm (hidari age uke) at a 45-degree angle to the previous block. Shout a loud "kiai!"

55. Draw back your left foot so that it is level with your right foot.

56. Finish in the yame, or finishing position.

heian nidan: summary

The main movements of the heian nidan kata are shown here without the transitional movements as a quick reference guide.

1. Ready stance.

2. Quarter-turn, double block.

3. Close punch.

4. Middle hammer-fist strike.

5. Half-turn, double block.

6. Close punch.

7. Middle hammer-fist strike.

8. Quarter-turn, side kick.

9. Half-turn, knife-hand guarding block.

10. Knife-hand guarding block.

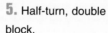

11. Knife-hand guarding block.

12. Spear-finger thrust with "kiai!"

13. Three-quarter-turn, knife-hand guarding block.

14. 45-degree turn, knife-hand guarding block.

15. 135-degree turn, knife-hand guarding block.

16. 145-degree turn, knife-hand guarding block.

17. 45-degree turn, press, followed by reverse outer block.

18. Front kick.

19. Reverse punch.

20. Outer block.

21. Front kick.

22. Reverse punch.

23. Augmented block.

24. Quarter-turn, lower block.

25. 45-degree turn, upper block.

26. 135-degree turn, lower block.

27. 45-degree turn, upper block with "kiai!"

28. Finishing position.

applications for heian nidan
application number 1

The spear-finger thrust, or nukite, is delivered in a similar way to a punch. However, as you can imagine, it is far less powerful! To execute the attack properly, you must be very precise and understand where the target is.

Note how the fingers are pointing toward the clavicular notch at the bottom of the throat. Place your finger on your own throat, and you'll understand how painful a full strike would be!

Movement number 23 from the heian nidan kata.

application number 2

In tournaments, grabbing clothing is forbidden. However, kata applications are not the same as tournament techniques. Here the grab gives an extra dimension, that of control.

Look at the photograph below. Note how the ball of the foot is being used to kick into the lower section of the abdominal region.

Movement number 36 from the heian nidan kata.

fourth kata: heian sandan

The levels of the "peaceful mind" described for the katas so far by no means reflect the requirements of the individual kata. Just because you are working on one of the earlier katas, it does not mean that you can allow your mind to wander. My suggestions, gained from insights into the martial arts, may help you to unify your mind and body in the movement of the katas.

In heian sandan, there is much call for the synchronization of different parts of the body. The technique of kosa uke, a blocking technique introduced here, is impossible to perform well without a good level of coordination.

This is another level of the peaceful mind. If you can stop the flow of random thoughts in your mind, it is easier to coordinate the different parts of your body with your mind.

Heian sandan introduces kosa uke, a stamping kick, an elbow block, a reverse elbow, and a vertical punch.

The full kata, including transitional moves, is explained first. A quick reference summary is provided on pages 202 to 203.

1. Assume the yoi, or ready position.

2. Step across with your left leg into the back stance. Cross your arms in front of your body.

3. Execute the inside forearm block to the midsection (hidari chudan uchi uke).

4. Leaving your left fist where it is, step up with your right foot so that your feet are parallel. Point your right fist downward.

5. Swap the position of your fists from high to low in a snapping motion for kosa uke.

6. Snap down your right fist and jab upward with your left fist for a second kosa uke.

7. Slide back your right foot ready for the back stance and cross your arms in front of your body (left arm on top).

8. Twist into the back stance and execute an inside forearm block to the midsection for migi chudan uchi uke.

9. Leaving your right fist where it is, step up with your left foot so that your feet are parallel. Point your left fist downward.

10. Swap the position of your fists from high to low in a snapping motion for kosa uke.

11. Snap down your left fist and jab your right fist upward for a final kosa uke.

12. Step across with your left foot ready for a back stance. Cross your arms in front of your body.

13. Execute the augmented block, with your left arm supported by your right, in the back stance.

14. Step through with your right foot in preparation for the front stance. Prepare your hands for the spear finger.

15. Execute the spear-finger thrust with your right hand (migi shihon nukite) in the front stance.

16. Shift your weight onto your left leg as you twist your body. Rotate your arm so that your thumb points down.

17. Step out with your left leg into a sideways horse-riding stance and whip your left fist around for a bottom-of-fist strike (hidari tettsui uchi).

Side view.

18. Step through with your right leg in preparation for the front stance. Leave your left arm extended in preparation for the following punch.

19. Front-punch to the midsection (migi chudan oi zuki) in the front stance with a loud "kiai!"

20. Step up into the ryoken koshi gamae, with your fists slightly above your belt.

Side view.

Front view.

21. Keep your fists in position and swing your right foot upward for a crescent kick.

22. Finish the crescent kick with a right elbow block (migi empi uke).

Front view.

Front view.

23. Release your right fist in preparation for a back-fist strike.

24. Execute a high back-fist strike (jodan uraken uchi).

Front view.

25. Bring your fist back to your belt.

26. Keeping your fists in position, swing your left foot upward for a crescent kick.

27. Finish the crescent kick with a left elbow block (hidari empi uke).

28. Release your left fist in preparation for a back fist.

29. Execute a high back-fist strike (hidari uraken uchi).

30. Move your left fist to the area of your belt.

31. Keeping your fists in position, swing your right foot upward for a crescent kick.

32. Finish the crescent kick with a right elbow block (migi empi uke).

33. Release your right fist in preparation for a back-fist strike.

Front view.

34. Execute a high back-fist strike (jodan uraken uchi).

35. Bring your right fist back again.

36. Move your right hand to your left hip.

Front view.

Front view.

37. Slowly move your right hand across for a vertical knife-hand block (migi chudan tate shuto uke).

38. Move your left leg next to your right leg.

Front view

39. Execute a forward punch to the midsection with your left fist (hidari chudan oi zuki) in the front stance.

40. Step up with your right leg into a parallel stance.

41. Pivot your right foot around by swinging your left leg through a half-turn into a wide horse-riding stance.

42. Execute a right vertical punch over your left shoulder and a reverse elbow strike with your left elbow (migi tate zuki hidari empi).

43. Do a left vertical punch over your right shoulder and a reverse elbow strike with your right elbow (hidari tate zuki hidari empi) with a "kiai!"

44. Step across with your right foot to make a narrower stance ready for the yame, or finishing position. Cross your arms.

45. Snap down your arms into the yame, or finishing, position.

heian sandan: summary

The main movements of the heian sandan kata are shown here without the transitional movements as a quick reference guide.

1. Ready stance.

2. Quarter-turn, inside forearm block.

3. Kosa uke.

4. Kosa uke.

5. Half-turn, inside forearm block.

6. Kosa uke.

7. Kosa uke.

8. Quarter-turn, augmented block.

9. Spear-finger thrust.

10. Hammer-fist strike.

11. Punch with "kiai!"

12. Half-turn, ryoken koshi gamae.

13. Elbow block.

14. Back fist.

15. Half-turn, elbow block.

16. Back fist.

17. Half-turn, elbow block.

18. Back fist.

19. Vertical knife-hand block.

20. Punch.

21. Half-turn, vertical punch, and reverse elbow strike.

22. Side-step, vertical punch, and reverse elbow strike with "kiai!"

23. Finishing position.

applications for heian sandan
application number 1

This photograph shows the crescent kick being used as a sparring technique. Instead of hitting the opponent with the heel, the flat of the foot is used. This is more like a slapping action with the foot, but can still be very powerful!

Movement number 21 from the heian sandan kata.

application number 2

This photograph shows an escape from a grab from behind.

1	**Your attacker grabs you from behind.**
2	**Strike your attacker's solar plexus with your elbow.**
3	**Twist around and strike your attacker's chin, as shown here.**

Movement number 42 from the heian sandan kata.

fifth kata: heian yondan

If you have been training for long enough to start learning this kata for your grading, it means that you are no longer in the beginner's group. You will have gained much in terms of physical fitness and coordination.

As you approach the more advanced techniques and concepts, there is one thing that overrides all other aspects: spirit. If you watch the high-grade karateka in your club performing their kata, there should be something very powerful about their performance: the spirit that they put into it. Try to think about how you can inject more spirit into your own performance.

The full heian yondan kata, including transitional moves, is explained first. A reference summary is provided on pages 216 to 218.

1. Step across with your left leg into the back stance and make knife hands below the level of your belt.

2. Raise your arms into the back-arm-block position (haishu haiwan uke) with a slow inhalation taking four to five seconds.

3. Drop your hands below your belt again and transfer your weight to your left leg so that you are facing the other way in the back stance.

4. Raise your arms into the back-arm-block position (haishu haiwan uke) with a slow inhalation taking four to five seconds.

5. Step across with your left leg, bringing your left foot close to your right. Keeping your hands high, move your right arm across your body.

6. Step forward in the front stance and thrust your fists in front of your body so that your forearms cross for the X–block (gedan juji uke).

7. Step up with your right leg and allow your body to turn so that your right forearm is above your left.

8. Step forward in the back stance and execute the augmented block (morote uke) with your right arm.

9. Draw your left foot close to your right and pull your left hand back to your belt.

10. Simultaneously execute the side-snapping kick with your left leg and a back-fist strike with your left fist.

11. Extend your left hand.

12. Step forward in the front stance to deliver a front elbow attack with your right elbow (migi mae empi).

13. Simultaneously execute a side-snapping kick with your right leg and a back-fist strike with your right fist (yoko keage uraken uchi).

14. Extend your right hand.

15. Step forward in the front stance to deliver a front elbow attack with your left elbow (migi mae empi).

16. Open your hands.

17. Strike downward with your left hand in a knife hand to the lower level (hidari gedan shuto barai). Your right hand protects your head.

18. Lower your right hand and raise your left as you begin to twist your body for the next strike.

19. Twist forward in the front stance as you deliver a high-section, right-hand, side knife-hand strike. Your left hand protects your head.

20. Raise your right knee to get ready for a front kick.

21. Execute a front kick to head height with your right leg (migi jodan mae geri).

22. Lower your foot.

23. Lower your foot and raise your right fist.

24. Step forward with your right leg into the front stance.

25. Perform a midsection, back-fist strike with a "kiai!"

26. Step back with your left leg.

27. Cross your forearms in front of your chest.

28. Slowly exhale and release your arms into the wedge block.

29. Raise your knee, ready for a front kick.

30. Execute a front kick with your right foot.

31. Lower your foot.

32. Step down into the front stance to perform a midsection punch.

33. Prepare to perform a reverse punch.

34. Execute a reverse punch.

35. Draw your right foot inward.

36. Cross your arms in front of your chest.

37. Slowly exhale as you release your arms.

38. Release your arms into a middle wedge block.

39. Raise your left knee, ready for a front kick.

40. Execute a front kick with your left foot.

41. Lower your foot.

42. Step down into the front stance and perform a middle punch.

43. Prepare to execute a reverse punch.

44. Execute a reverse punch with your right fist.

45. Step forward in the back stance and lower your arms.

46. Perform an augmented left block in the back stance.

47. Step forward in the front stance and prepare to make a double-handed grabbing attack.

48. Perform an augmented right block in the back stance.

49. Step forward in the back stance and lower your arms.

50. Perform an augmented left block in the back stance.

51. Step forward in the front stance and prepare to perform a double-handed grabbing attack.

52. Execute a high double-handed grabbing attack in the front stance.

53. Start to pull down your hands as you begin to raise your right knee.

54. Pull down your hands as you sharply raise your knee for a knee kick.

55. Pivot on your left foot as you prepare to block with your arms.

56. Come down into the back stance to perform a midsection knife-hand block with your left hand.

57. Perform a midsection knife-hand block with your right hand.

58. Assume the finishing position, or yame.

heian yondan: summary

The main movements of the heian yondan kata are shown here without the transitional movements as a quick reference guide.

1. Ready stance.

2. Quarter-turn, back arm block.

3. Half-turn, back arm block.

4. Quarter-turn, low X-block.

5. Augmented block.

6. Side-snap kick with back-fist strike.

7. Front elbow strike.

8. Half-turn, side-snap kick with back fist.

9. Front elbow strike.

10. Lower knife hand.

11. Quarter-turn, upper knife hand.

12. Front kick.

13. Pressing block.

14. Back fist with "kiai!"

15. Half-turn, middle wedge block.

16. Front kick.

17. Punch.

18. Reverse punch.

19. Quarter-turn, middle wedge block.

20. Front kick.

21. Front punch.

22. Reverse punch.

23. Augmented block. **24.** Augmented block. **25.** High grab with both hands. **26.** Knee kick with "kiai!"

27. Half-turn, knife-hand block. **28.** Knife-hand block. **29.** Finishing position.

applications for heian yondan
application number 1

The heian yondan kata employs the side kick.
Be sure to keep your balance while kicking,
as demonstrated here.

Movement number 11 from the
heian yondan kata, the side kick.

application number 2

Knees can be very effective when used as
weapons. In this application, the opponent's
head is also brought to the knee, doubling the
effect.

Movement number 54 from the
heian yondan kata, the knee kick.

sixth kata: heian godan

The heian godan kata is the final kata that we will look at here. If you have reached this kata in your grading, you have achieved a good level of understanding. You are over halfway to a black belt; karate will start to become even more interesting!

There is a concept associated with this kata called the "flowing-water" technique. This concept can be interpreted in many ways. One interpretation is to think about how water behaves. If there is a gap, water will flow into it. It does not think about the gap and automatically assumes the right shape to fill it.

Sparring can be similar at a high level. If there is a gap in your opponent's defense, it will normally close if you spend any time at all thinking about it. If you can sense the gap with your inner ki, you will automatically flow into it using the right technique. You will have bypassed the stage where you need to think about what you are going to do. Reaching this level takes a lot of practice!

This kata includes the high X-block, lower spear-finger thrust, and "jumping over the bo." A bo is a traditional Japanese weapon; it is basically a long, wooden staff.

The full kata, including transitional moves, is explained first. A quick reference summary is provided on pages 230 to 232.

1. Start in the yoi, or ready, position.

2. Step across with your left leg and cross your arms.

3. Go into the back stance; snap out your left arm for a left middle outer block. Make knife hands below your belt.

4. Stay in the back stance, keep your feet still, and prepare for a reverse punch.

5. Execute a reverse punch with your right fist (migi chudan gyaku zuki).

6. Slide your right foot forward and let your right fist drop as you turn your body.

7. On a long inhalation, draw your feet together for a hidari kagi gamae.

8. Slide your right foot forward into the back stance and cross your arms in front of your body.

9. Snap your arms open for an outer forearm block made with your right arm (migi chudan uke).

10. Draw back your left elbow for a reverse punch.

11. Perform a reverse punch with your left fist (hidari chudan gyaku zuki) without moving your feet.

12. Pull your left foot closer to your right as you step up into the higher stance.

13. Bring both feet together on a long inhalation for migi kaje gamae.

14. Step forward into the back stance.

15. Perform an augmented block with your right arm (migi chudan morote uke).

16. Step forward with your left foot and cross your arms in front of your body.

17. Twist forward as you press into the front stance for a low X-block (gedan juji uke).

18. Pull back your elbows.

19. Do a high X-block with knife hands (jodan juji uke).

20. Pull your hands to your right side.

21. Perform a pressing block (chudan osae uke).

22. Step up with your right leg as you perform a left, vertical knife-hand block (hidari chidan tate shuto uke), ready to punch with your right hand.

23. Step into the front stance as you prepare to punch.

24. Perform a forward punch to the midsection with your right hand (chudan migi oi zuki) and shout a "kiai!"

25. Swing your right foot around in a 180-degree turn.

26. Execute a crescent kick to head height.

27. Control your leg before landing.

28. Land in the horse-riding stance with a low block (migi gedan barai).

29. Cross your arms in front of your chest.

30. On a long inhalation, execute a middle back-hand strike (chudan haishu uke).

31. Swing your right leg for a crescent kick and extend your left palm.

32. At the high point of the crescent kick, the sole of your foot should slap into the palm of your hand.

33. Turn through a right angle in the horse-riding stance and extend your left palm.

34. Perform an elbow strike with your right elbow (migi mae empi).

35. Start moving into the reverse cat stance and cross your arms in front of your chest.

36. Perform a right-hand-side, midsection augmented block (migi chudan morote uke).

37. Turn your body.

38. Stand with your feet together and your arms held high.

39. Jump high in the air as you turn through a right angle and shout a loud "kiai!"

40. Land with your weight on your right as you perform an X-block with a "kiai!"

41. Step across with your right leg and drop your arms.

42. Twist your body around in the front stance for an augmented block.

43. Step across with your left leg. Raise your right arm and lower your left.

44. Prepare for a low spear-finger strike.

45. Twist your body into the front stance and thrust your right hand forward.

46. Step across with your left foot into the back stance.

47. Perform a low block with your left fist and raise your right fist.

48. Pull your left foot closer to your right foot.

49. Turn your body through 180 degrees and raise your right arm.

50. Block downward with your right arm and raise your left (manji gamae in heisoku dachi).

51. Step across with your right leg and open your hands.

52. Twist into the front stance and thrust your left hand forward for a spear-finger strike (hidari gedan shuto uchi).

53. Step across with your left foot into the back stance.

54. Perform a low block with your right hand while raising your left hand (manji gamae).

55. Step back and across with your right leg as you cross your arms in front of your chest.

56. Assume the finishing, or yame, stance.

heian godan summary

The main movements of the heian godan kata are shown here without the transitional movements as a quick reference guide.

1. Ready position.

2. Quarter-turn, outer forearm block.

3. Reverse punch.

4. Long breath, into the attention stance.

5. Quarter-turn, outer forearm block.

6. Reverse punch.

7. Long breath, into the attention stance.

8. Quarter-turn, augmented block.

9. Low X-block.

10. High X-block.

11. Pressing block.

12. Punch with "kiai!"

13. Low block.

14. Middle back-hand strike.

15. Right crescent kick.

16. Right front elbow strike.

17. Right middle augmented block.

18. Raise fists, attention stance.

19. Jump with "kiai!"

20. Augmented block.

21. Low spear-finger thrust.

22. Attention stance.

23. Half-turn, attention stance.

24. Quarter-turn, low spear-finger thrust.

25. Low block.

90. Finishing position.

This kata is supposed to flow like water.

applications for heian godan
application number 1

Another application of the arm-locking techniques used in karate.

This is movement 7 of the heian godan kata, hidari kagi gamae.

application number 2

The crescent kick can be used as a powerful attack. This is shown later in the kata.

1	**Block the attack with the open hand.**
2	**Strike the face with a crescent kick.**
3	**Follow the attack with a front elbow strike.**

One of the useful things about the kata is that you can train on your own. You can work a little each day on the kata and then ask your sensei to correct any perceived imperfections.

This way of training on your own is very one-dimensional, however, and is certainly not what the spirit of karate is all about. To understand a technique, you need to practice it with somebody else. Practicing your karate with a partner is called kumite, or sparring.

Kumite is performed on different levels. The first level is five-step sparring. In this, the karateka make five steps. Each step is an attack by one partner, with the receiving partner delivering a counterattack on the final attack. This approach teaches the karateka how to distance themselves and become accustomed to the idea of an attacker.

The next stage is three-step sparring. Three-step sparring follows the same pattern as five-step sparring, except that there are three steps instead of five. It is really a development of five-step sparring, and gives the karateka the chance to demonstrate more techniques in less time.

The final part of the choreographed sparring sequences is one-step sparring. In one-step sparring, one karateka attacks the other, who responds with a known technique. The emphasis here is on speed and accuracy.

Both karateka will know these choreographed sequences. There will be no contact, but the attacks and defenses will be executed as though they were real. The fact that both karateka know what is going on gives them the chance to use maximum speed and power.

The final aspect of sparring is free sparring, or jiyu kumite. In jiyu kumite, the karateka try to attack each other in order to score points. Jiyu kumite gives the karateka the chance to test themselves. It is an excellent technique for sharpening skills, and the technique that is used for sport karate.

We will now examine some examples of the different sparring levels.

five-step sparring: gohon kumite

Apart from practicing applications from the kata, gohon kumite is the first chance that a karateka has to practice his or her skills with another person. For this reason, the attacks are usually fairly straightforward.

That having been said, do not think that it can look sloppy. The spirit should be strong for both karateka. There should be a good "kiai!" on the retaliation at the end of the sequence, and both karateka should maintain a high level of mental alertness and fighting spirit.

Do not make the mistake of walking through the practice with no real intent. Each punch should be performed as though it were real.

1. Start in yoi, the ready stance.

2. Bow.

3. Yoi (your partner should remain in yoi).

4. Step into the front stance; do a low block.

5. As your partner punches low, block with a low block. As your partner steps forward, step back. (Step one.)

 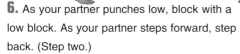

6. As your partner punches low, block with a low block. As your partner steps forward, step back. (Step two.)

7. As your partner punches low, block with a low block. As your partner steps forward, step back. (Step three.)

8. As your partner punches low, block with a low block. As your partner steps forward, step back. (Step four.)

9. As your partner punches low, block with a high block. As your partner steps forward, step back. (Step five.)

10. Retaliate with a reverse-section punch to the mid-section and shout "kiai!"

other variations

Your karate club will have a syllabus of five-step sparring that you will have to learn for your grading. This can vary, depending on the style of karate that you are practicing and who is teaching it. Some other common variations that you may want to try are these.

1. Steps with a low front kick and low block. Retaliate with a punch.

2. Steps with a middle punch and outer forearm block. Retaliate with a punch.

The list of variations could go on forever. Use your imagination!

three-step sparring: sambon kumite

The difference between sambon kumite and gohon kumite is that sambon kumite is performed on three different levels. This means that the attacks will be high, middle, and low.

The sequences are still prearranged. As with gohon kumite, clubs will have different sequences in their syllabbi. This example should be useful in giving you the gist of sambon kumite. It is always good to experiment, so try to make up your own sequences.

1. Start in yoi, the ready stance.

2. Bow.

3. Yoi (Steps 1 and 2 are only executed at the start of training with a new partner).

4. The attacker steps back in the front stance with a low block.

5. High punch with a high block. (Step one.)

6. Middle punch with an inner forearm block. (Step two.)

7. Front kick with a low block. (Step three.)

8. Retaliate with a reverse middle punch and a shout of "kiai!"

one-step sparring: kihon ippon kumite

The last of the fixed kumite sequences is usually kihon ippon kumite, or one-step sparring. In kihon ippon kumite, we are still following a set sequence. That is, both karateka know exactly what is going to happen.

The concept is straightforward. Your partner attacks with a known technique that you will either evade or block. Then you will retaliate with another known technique.

Four examples follow.

example number 1

A high punch is deflected with an upper block. The retaliation is a reverse, midsection punch.

1. Start in yoi, the ready stance.

2. Your attacker steps back into the front stance with a low block.

3. Your attacker starts to step into a high punch. Prepare to step back for a high block.

4. The high punch is deflected with a high block. Retaliate with a reverse punch.

example number 2

A high punch is deflected with an upper X–block. Retaliate with a turning kick to the attacker's solar plexus.

In retaliations to the midsection, very light contact is desirable.

In crisp, sharp retaliations to the high section, no contact should be made.

1. Assume the yoi, or ready, stance.

2. Your attacker punches. You block with an X-block.

3. Control the attacker's arm by pulling it down.

4. Use your right hand to keep control of the attacker's wrist and retaliate with a roundhouse kick to the solar plexus.

example number 3

A low front kick is deflected with a lower block. The retaliation is made with a reverse punch to the attacker's midsection.

1. Assume the yoi, or ready, stance.

2. Your attacker executes a front kick. You evade by stepping into a long front stance and executing a right-hand downward block.

3. When the kick lands, you will be behind your attacker.

4. Retaliate with a reverse punch to your attacker's kidneys or spine.

example number 4

A high turning kick is deflected with a twin knife-hand block.

The retaliation is made with an elbow strike to the midsection. Counterattack by coming in close for an elbow strike to the ribs.

1. Assume the yoi, or ready, stance.

2. The attacker steps back into the fighting stance.

3. The attacker starts to execute a roundhouse kick as you prepare to block.

4. The turning kick is blocked by the twin knife-hand block.

variation on kihon ippon kumite

A variation that is taught for kihon ippon kumite is jiyu ippon kumite. It works in much the same way as kihon ippon kumite, except that the attacks and retaliations are not pre-determined. It is semi-freestyle one-step sparring.

In jiyu ippon kumite, the attacker decides if he or she will attack low, middle, or high, and the technique to use. The defender must then use an appropriate block followed by an effective attack. The aim of this type of sparring is to get away from the choreographed style of attack and become more free-flowing.

5. Follow through with an elbow strike to the attacker's ribs.

free sparring: jiyu kumite

So far, all of the patterns and sparring techniques that we have looked at have been choreographed in one way or another. The purpose of so much choreographed work is to program a set of responses into your body and mind. Then, if an attack comes, you do not need to think about what to do, you just do it.

Free sparring is an aspect of karate in which you test your responses. In free sparring, you have the opportunity to test your skills.

Free sparring is not a free-for-all. To avoid injury, we must follow very strict guidelines. Respect for your training partner is paramount. Under no circumstances should a fighter lose control. Karateka who become angry and try to hurt an opponent are showing how little they understand about their training!

Always bow first.

Free sparring is popular because it can be used as a sport. This can lead karateka in a dangerous direction. By definition, sport has winners and losers: it is all about competition.

To want to "beat" your training partner in a sparring situation means that you want to be the best in some way. This is an ego issue, and a common phrase in martial arts is, "When you enter the dojo, leave your ego at the door."

If you are sparring and your partner gets through your defenses, this is actually a good thing. Think about it. How did it happen? Can he or she do it the next time? How do I stop him or her? Every time that your partner penetrates your defenses, he or she has taught you something. Try not to let your ego get in the way and stop you from learning it!

Adopt the fighting stance.

free sparring

In a karate class, the most advanced form of free sparring is when two karateka are simulating a fight situation in a continuous practice fight. This is very different to real fighting in that there are rules. These rules are essential for the safety of the karateka. It is a mark of respect to both your fellow karateka and all that has gone before you in karate that you do not break the rules.

The rules of sparring vary from club to club, but essentially follow this concept.

Performed with respect for your fellow karateka, free sparring is an energetic and highly enjoyable way of learning karate. Just remember: you are there to *learn*, not to win.

Here are some images of free sparring.

1	No strikes below the belt.
2	No strikes to vital areas, such as the neck, kidneys, or groin.
3	No strikes to the joints (elbows or knees).
4	No excessive contact.
5	No strikes to the head, unless headgear is worn.
6	Always wear groin protection and a mouthguard.
7	Show respect for your partner. If you are more advanced than him or her, this is not an excuse for you to give your partner a bad time.
8	If the instructor shouts "yame," you must immediately stop what you are doing. This rule is extremely important and overrides anything else that may be happening in the dojo.

Turning kick.   Followed by a back kick.   Another turning kick performed with the other leg.

Retaliate with a high turning kick.

And another one.

Follow through with a lunge punch.

Attack with a spear-finger thrust.

Retaliate with a jumping front kick.

Fight back with another lunge punch.

Retaliate with a lunge punch.

Execute a hooking punch.

Retaliate with an elbow strike.

learning techniques for sparring

When you start to learn free sparring, you will usually be in a situation where there are more advanced karateka than you in the lesson. They are there to help you. They will remember what it feels like to be a beginner, and how ferocious a high-section side kick can look.

Use the situation. Remember that a more advanced student will not be perfect either. If you see an opening, take it, but keep your control. A frequent mistake that a beginner makes is to see an opening and not to show control. Remember that your sparring partners may have some tricks left up the sleeves of their gis!

As well as free sparring, the following two exercises are commonly used when practicing sparring.

First, only one person attacking and the other only blocking. This is a practice technique in which one karateka is on the attack and the other is only allowed to defend. The attacker knows that he or she is in no danger of being attacked, so can build up speed for the attack. This forces the defender to be very sharp when evading and defending.

Second, one-for-one free sparring. This is very similar to normal free sparring. As long as you stay within the rules of your dojo for sparring, you are encouraged to use any suitable technique. The difference is that you take turns attacking. This is an excellent way of building up speed and stamina.

the karate tournament

Tournaments have always been part of martial arts. In the old days, martial-arts tournaments were frequently held as spectator events at festivals. They gave the master the chance to show his students to the world, and the students the chance to display their skills. If a tournament went well, the master's reputation was enhanced, along with that of his students.

Some martial arts like aikido do not really lend themselves to tournaments, and tournaments are therefore not a normal part of the training routine. With its grace and power, karate can make the ideal spectator sport, however.

In modern times, tournaments have become more important in karate, and styles that are similar to karate, than they have ever been before. If karateka enter a tournament with the correct attitude, then the tournament can be a valuable opportunity to meet people and learn more about your skill. It is sometimes good to see how you perform under pressure!

If you enter a tournament with the attitude that you are going to do your best, but that winning is not important, you will gain much from the tournament. If you enter with the idea that you must win at all costs, your ego is talking to you. If you are in this state of mind, you will miss out on many of the lessons that you could otherwise have learned.

It is useful to enter a tournament every now and then because it focuses your training wonderfully. If you know that you will be entering a tournament in three months' time, you will not miss many training sessions!

A negative consequence could be entering too many tournaments. This could result in a karateka who looks good in a tournament situation, but has very little of the deeper understanding that is a part of karate.

There are many different governing bodies and karate associations. Most of them hold tournaments of some kind. You will find that the rules vary between tournaments. It is therefore of little use to try to explain competition rules in detail because we could only ever cover the details of one of thousands of tournaments.

My advice to any karateka is to attend a karate tournament, even if you only go as a spectator. It is a part of the karate world that can be very interesting.

types of tournaments

In karate, there are two main categories of tournaments. These are the kata, or patterns, category and the kumite, or sparring, section. There follows a review of both.

kata tournaments

In a kata tournament, you will perform your kata in front of a panel of judges. Depending on the type of tournament, the kata can either be one that you choose or one that the competition rules dictate. You will always know which kata you will be demonstrating well in advance.

A more modern version of the kata tournament goes under the name "creative kata." For creative kata, the karateka will have devised their own kata. Sometimes these kata are even set to music.

The judges will be looking for qualities like spirit, timing, correctness of the kata, and good technique. Each will give a score, in a similar way to an Olympic ice-skating event. The karateka with the highest score is the winner.

In kata competitions, you will usually be split between juniors and adults, with another split between grades. The grading split will normally have two or three splits up to the first kyu, and then the dan grades together, but this may vary.

Kata competition demands good focus. On the day of your tournament, you will naturally feel a little nervous. This anxiety is increased by the knowledge that you are being judged by your peers in front of an audience. Staying focused despite that amount of pressure will at least prove that you have learned focus!

kumite tournaments

In a kumite competition, you will be sparring against people who are roughly the same grade and weight as you. There is also a split between adults and younger sparring partners.

You may, or may not, know your sparring partner, depending on the size of the tournament. It is possible for some students from the better clubs to meet their normal sparring partners in the finals. This usually makes for an interesting finish!

In karate, the rules usually dictate that the strikes should be pulled. This means that if your contact is deemed to be excessive by the judges, you could be disqualified.

The sparring area will be covered with training mats. There will be a panel of judges, a referee, and corner judges. Someone who knows first aid will always be present. There will be a medical doctor present at the tournament, too.

Points are won for clean techniques. Points may be deducted for bad conduct. A referee may disqualify you from a match for bad conduct. The referee's decision is always final for all aspects of the bout.

The duration of the bouts can vary. A typical bout consists of two three-minute rounds. It may not sound like much, but I can assure you that it feels like a long time when you are on the mats!

The bouts are usually performed as qualifiers, quarterfinals, semifinals, and finals. The winner is the karateka who gets through all of them undefeated.

conclusion: so what *is* karate?

By this stage, you should have learned something about karate that has increased your understanding of karate's scope and definition. We have seen that it has many aspects that can all be expressed in different ways.

So what is karate? Is it a fitness system? A fighting system? A method for spiritual growth? A good way of defending yourself?

For a definition, let's look to someone who had a good idea, the founder of karate: Gichin Funakoshi. He once described karate as being like a mirror.

If you are preoccupied with violence, then you will see karate as a violent art form. If fitness is what you seek, you will see karate as a fitness session. If you are intent on spiritual growth, you will see karate as a vehicle for that growth.

Think about how you view the karate that you practice. Do you see yourself becoming more fit or more dangerous, or working on your spirit? You cannot fool yourself because the only person who knows the real answer is you.

Just as we use a mirror in the bathroom to look at our exteriors, so we can use karate to view our interiors. If you can see what is going on inside, you can work on changing it if you need to do so. In this way, karate is an invaluable aid for learning more about yourself.

And in a way, that idea fits with the Zen roots of karate because karate just *is*!

the Japanese language

Nobody expects you to become a linguist if you learn karate. But in many clubs, the names of the movements are called out in Japanese.

One of the reasons for this is that if you understand the Japanese name of a technique, then you will understand the name of that technique in whatever part of the world you are training in. So you can even practice karate on vacation!

Another good reason for being acquainted with the Japanese names is that karate is a traditional Japanese art. So why not learn the names that karate itself has given its techniques rather than those given to them by an interpreter?

NUMBERS

1	**One**	ich
2	**Two**	ni
3	**Three**	san
4	**Four**	chi
5	**Five**	go
6	**Six**	roku
7	**Seven**	sichi
8	**Eight**	hachi
9	**Nine**	ku
10	**Ten**	jyu
11	**Eleven**	jyu-ich
12	**Twelve**	jyu-ni
20	**Twenty**	nijyu
30	**Thirty**	sanjyu
40	**Forty**	yonjyu
50	**Fifty**	gojyu

As you can see from eleven and twelve, if you want a higher number than a multiple of ten, use the multiple of ten with the lower digit. So, for example, thirteen will be jyu-san.

TECHNIQUES

Age uke	upward block
Ai	harmony
Aikido	a Japanese martial art based on harmonizing with the opponent's energy
Bo	a wooden staff for fighting with
Cha	tea
Choku zuki	straight punch
Chudan	middle
Dachi	stance
Dan	black-belt grade
Do	the way
Dojo	training hall
Empi	elbow
Empi uchi	elbow strike
Gedan	lower
Gedan barai	downward block
Gedan juji uke	X-block
Geri	kick
Gi	a white outfit worn by karate students and their teachers
Goju-ryu	the hard–soft way (a karate style)
Gyaku zuki	reverse punch
Hachiji dachi	natural stance
Haito uchi	ridge-hand strike
Haiwan uke	back arm block
Hara	the physical and energy center of your body
Heian	peaceful mind
Hidari	left
Hiza geri uchi	knee kick
Jiyu kumite	free sparring
Jodan	upper
Judo	a Japanese martial art based on locks and throws
Ju-jitsu	A martial art based on the ways of the samurai

Kage zuki	hooking punch
Kakiwake uke	wedge block
Kan	hall
Karate	"the way of the empty hand"
Karateka	a student of karate
Kata	a sequence of movement designed to teach the basics of the karate style
Ki	the "vital energy" inherent in everything
Kiai	the karate yell
Kiba dachi	straddle stance
Kihon	basics
Kimae	breath control
Kizami zuki	jabbing punch
Koken	hook hand
Kokutsu dachi	back stance
Kumite	sparring
Kyu	grades away from black belt
Mae geri	front kick
Makiwara	striking block for conditioning parts of the body
Mawashi geri	roundhouse kick
Migi	right
Mikazuki geri	crescent kick
Morote uke	augmented block
Neko ashi dachi	cat stance
Nukite	spear finger
Ochi uke	pressing block
Oi zuki	stepping punch
Okinawa	an island near Japan
Rei	bow
Samurai	the old warrior caste of Japan
Sensei	a teacher; "one who shows the way"
Shiatsu	a Japanese healing art using pressure to alter the flow of ki
Shuto uchi	inside knife-hand strike

Shuto uke	knife-hand block
Soto shuto uchi	outside knife-hand strike
Soto ude uke	outer forearm block
Tate shuto uke	vertical knife-hand block
Te	empty hand
Teisho uchi	palm-heel strike
Tettsui uchi	hammer-fist strike
Tobikonde mae geri	jumping front kick
Tsubo	pressure point
Uchi	strike
Uchi ude uke	inner forearm block
Uke	block
Uraken uchi	back fist strike
Ushiro chudan empi uchi	reverse middle elbow strike
Ushiro geri	back kick
Ushiro mawashi geri	reverse roundhouse kick
Wado ryu	"the way of harmony," a karate style
Yama zuki	"U" punch
Yame	finish
Yoi	attention
Yoko geri keage	side-snap kick
Zen	meditation
Zenkutsu dachi	front stance
Zuki	punch

index

bibliography and credits
bibliography

John Van Weenen,

The Beginner's Guide to Shotokan Karate (1983).

Michael J Alter,

Sport Stretching (1990).

Fulcher and Fox,

Your Personal Trainer (2002).

To all those who have helped me to take steps along the path of knowledge in the martial and healing arts, and most of all to my wife, Carol, for the love and patience that she has shown me while taking that path.

credits

The author and publishers would like to thank the following people for taking part in this book.

John Hurley (1): sensei, 3rd dan wado ryu. Other styles: shotokan karate, 1st dan.

John started training in wado ryu karate in south-east London, England, in 1999. He reached 3rd kyu in four years under Sensei Fellows of Renga Higashi. He switched to shotokan karate in 1988, and was awarded his black belt in 1991. He traded in his 1st dan in shotokan for a 3rd kyu in higashi, and has been training in higashi ever since. John also has experience in a number of other martial arts, such as muay Thai boxing (under Master Chris Price), shaolin kung fu (under Sifu Rob Simpson) and wing chun kung fu (under Sifu Alan Legg).

Glenn Stevens (2): Glenn is one of the few professional full-time martial-arts instructors in Britain, and has been training and teaching for over fifteen years. He is currently a 3rd dan in shotokan karate. As a former national champion, Glenn has competed nationally and internationally with great success. He has trained with many of the top masters in the martial arts, and has continued to develop his martial-arts and teaching skills. He has also recently been certified to teach arnis de mano Filipino weapons' systems.

Sam Wright (3): 2nd kyu. Other styles: tang soo do, 3rd kyu; judo, 5th kyu; kickboxing, 7th kyu.

Sam started martial arts at the age of nine, studying judo. After three years, she changed her style to tang soo do, training under Grandmaster Lee (9th dan) for two-and-a-half years. She gained her 3rd kyu and enjoyed competition success by winning the bronze medal for hyung (kata) and silver medal for fighting (non-contact) in the 1995 national championship. Since then, Sam has been practicing higashi alone, and achieved her brown belt in just one year.

1   2   3